THE CAKE MIX BIBLE

Publications International, Ltd.

Favorite Brand Name Recipes at www.fbnr.com

Microwave Cooking: Microwave ovens vary in wattage. Use the cooking times as guidelines and check for doneness before adding more time.

Preparation/Cooking Times: Preparation times are based on the approximate amount of time required to assemble the recipe before cooking, baking, chilling or serving. These times include preparation steps such as measuring, chopping and mixing. The fact that some preparations and cooking can be done simultaneously is taken into account. Preparation of optional ingredients and serving suggestions is not included.

contents

Introduction

Nothing could be easier than baking a cake using a cake mix. And with the right pan, a few additional ingredients and some decorating hints, you can transform that simple cake into a spectacular layer cake, a batch of delicious cookies, tasty bars or cute cupcakes, or even a decadent cheesecake.

The information that follows is designed to help you get started. It provides you with general baking tips, information on bakeware and ingredients, as well as professional decorating, garnishing and serving techniques.

getting started

Fabulous desserts and tempting treats start with good baking habits. Keep the following techniques in mind when you're ready to start baking.

- Read the entire recipe before beginning to make sure you have all the necessary ingredients, utensils and supplies.

- For the best results, use the ingredients called for in the recipe.

- Remove butter, margarine and cream cheese from the refrigerator to soften, if necessary.

- Complete any prep work, such as toasting or chopping nuts, peeling and slicing fruit or melting chocolate or butter before actually beginning to make the recipe.

- Measure all of the ingredients accurately and assemble them in the order they are called for in the recipe.

- Use the pan size that is specified in the recipe and prepare it according to the recipe directions.

- Adjust the oven racks and preheat the oven, if necessary. Check the oven temperature for accuracy with an oven thermometer.

- Follow recipe directions and baking times exactly. Check for doneness using the test given in the recipe. Begin testing a few minutes before the end of the specified baking time.

measuring

Dry Ingredients: Always use standardized measuring spoons and cups. Fill the appropriate measuring spoon or cup to overflowing and level it off with a metal spatula or the flat edge of a knife. When measuring flour, lightly spoon it into the measuring cup, then level it off. Do not tap or bang the measuring cup since this will pack the flour. If a recipe calls for "sifted flour," sift the flour before it is measured. If a recipe calls for "flour, sifted," measure the flour first and then sift. Dry measuring cups usually come in nested sets which include 1-cup, ½-cup, ⅓-cup and ¼-cup sizes.

Liquid Ingredients: Always use a standardized glass or plastic measuring cup with a pouring spout. Place the cup on a flat surface, fill to the desired mark and check the measurement at eye level. To make sure that sticky liquids, such as corn syrup, honey and molasses, won't cling to the measuring cup, lightly grease the cup with vegetable oil or spray it with nonstick cooking spray first before filling it. Liquid measuring cups are available in sizes anywhere from 1 cup to 4 cups, as well as 6-cup to 8-cup measuring bowls with pouring spouts.

baking pans

A **baking pan** is made of metal and has a square or rectangular shape with straight sides at least 1½ inches high. The most common sizes are 8 and 9 inches square; 11×7×2 inches; and 13×9×2 inches. Baking pans are designed for cakes and bar cookies. Shiny aluminum pans are ideal for producing a tender, lightly browned cake crust. Baking pans with dark finishes will absorb heat more quickly than shiny baking pans. When using baking pans with dark finishes or when substituting glass bakeware in recipes that call for baking pans, reduce the oven temperature by 25°F.

A **baking sheet** (often referred to as a cookie sheet) is a flat, rigid sheet of metal on which stiff dough is baked into cookies, rolls, biscuits, etc. It has a low lip on one or more sides for ease in handling; a lip higher than ½ inch will interfere with surface browning, especially of cookies. The type of surface also determines the browning characteristics of the baking sheet. Shiny finishes promote even browning. Dark metal baking sheets absorb more heat and cause food to brown more quickly. Insulated baking sheets have a layer of air sandwiched between two sheets of aluminum which helps to prevent excess browning but increases the baking time. (Some cookie doughs may also spread more on these types of baking sheets.) Nonstick finishes minimize sticking and make cleanup easier. Baking sheets vary in size. Before buying baking sheets, know the dimensions of your oven. A baking sheet should fit on an oven rack with at least one inch of space on all sides between the edge of the sheet and the oven wall. Without this space, heat circulation will be hampered.

A **bundt pan** is a fluted tube pan traditionally used to bake a densely textured bundt cake. Bundt pans usually measure 10 inches in diameter with a 12-cup capacity. They are traditionally made of cast aluminum with a nonstick interior coating but are also available in lightweight aluminum. Generously greasing the fluted sides is extremely important to prevent the cake from sticking.

A **cake pan** is a type of baking pan that is round with a straight side at least 1½ inches high. Pans made of aluminum or heavy-gauge steel produce a cake with a delicate, tender crust. Besides the most common round 8- or 9-inch cake pans, there is a wide array of pans available that measure from 3 to 24 inches in diameter. Cake pans also come in a variety of specialty shapes.

A **jelly-roll pan** is a rectangular baking pan with 1-inch-high sides. It is used to make a thin sponge cake that can be spread with jelly and rolled into a jelly roll. Jelly-roll pans are also used for making thin sheet cakes or bar cookies. Standard pans measure 15½×10½×1-inch. They are available in aluminum and steel. Jelly-roll pans are not a good choice for baking individual cookies, because the sides interfere with air circulation during baking, resulting in uneven browning.

Loaf pans are designed for baking yeast- and quick-bread loaves, pound cakes and fruit cakes. Standard pans measure 9×5×3 inches and have slightly flared sides. Small loaf pans measuring 8½×4½×2½ inches and mini pans measuring 5×4×2 inches are also available. Loaf pans come in a variety of materials including aluminum, steel and glass. Pans with dark exteriors are best for yeast breads. Those with shiny exteriors are best for quick breads and pound cakes.

Muffin pans are rectangular baking pans with 6 or 12 cup-shaped cavities. A standard muffin cup measures 2½ inches in diameter and 1½ inches deep. Also available are giant muffin pans with cups measuring 3¼ inches in diameter by 2 inches deep; and mini pans with cups measuring 1½ to 2 inches in diameter and ¾ inch deep. Muffin pans are made of aluminum, steel or cast iron.

A **springform pan** is a two-piece round baking pan with an expandable side (secured by a clamp or spring) and a removable bottom. When the clamp is opened, the rim expands and the bottom of the pan can be removed. This makes it easy to remove cheesecakes, cakes and tortes from the pan. The diameter ranges from 6 to 12 inches with 9- and 10-inch pans being the most common.

A **tube pan** is a round baking pan with a hollow tube in the center, which conducts heat to the center of the cake to promote even baking. The tube also supports delicate batters as they rise. Most tube pans have a high, slightly flared side. Some, such as angel food cake pans, have a removable bottom. They are usually 8 to 10 inches in diameter and 3½ to 4 inches high with a 12-cup capacity.

preparing pans

Grease baking pans and sheets only if directed to do so in the recipe. It is generally best to use vegetable shortening or nonstick vegetable spray to grease pans because butter and margarine can cause overbrowning at high oven temperatures. When baking pans are greased, the surface of the cake will be more tender. When baking pans are greased and floured, a slight crust will form on the cake which helps it release from the pan.

To **grease and flour** cake or baking pans, use a paper towel, waxed paper or your fingers to apply a thin, even layer of shortening. Sprinkle flour into the greased pan; shake or tilt the pan to coat evenly with flour, then tap lightly to remove any excess.

To **line pans** with waxed paper or parchment paper, trace the bottom of the pan onto a piece of waxed or parchment paper and cut it to fit. Grease the pan, but do not flour it. Press the paper onto the bottom of the greased pan.

Parchment paper is heavy paper that is impervious to grease and moisture. It is sold in sheets and in rolls. There are many uses for it in the kitchen, including making sealed envelopes for cooking *en papillote* and lining baking pans and sheets for cakes, cookies, meringues and cream puffs. It allows for easy removal of the baked goods from the pan. It also makes kitchen cleanup a breeze. It is available at gourmet kitchenware stores and at many supermarkets.

baking

- Adjust the oven racks. Oven racks may need to be set lower for cakes baked in tube pans.

- If two oven racks are used, arrange them so they divide the oven into thirds, then stagger the pans so they are not directly over each other.

- Preheat the oven to the desired temperature about 15 minutes before beginning to bake.

- Place the baking pan or sheet on the center rack of the oven. If two or more pans are used, allow at least an inch of space between the pans and two inches between the pans and the walls of the oven for proper heat circulation.

- If the heat distribution in your oven is uneven, turn the baking pan or sheet halfway through the baking time.

- Filled cake pans should be placed in the oven immediately after the batter is mixed. Cake batter should not sit before baking because chemical leaveners begin working as soon as they are mixed with liquids.

- Avoid opening the oven door during the first half of the baking time. The oven temperature must remain constant in order for a cake to rise properly.

- For even baking and browning of cookies, it is best to place only one baking sheet at a time in the center of the oven. However, if you must bake more than one sheet of cookies at a time, rotate them from the top rack to the bottom rack halfway through the baking time.

- Most cookies bake quickly and should be watched carefully to avoid overbaking. Check them at the minimum baking time, then watch carefully to make sure they don't burn. It is generally better to slightly underbake rather than to overbake cookies.

- When reusing the same baking sheets for several batches of cookies, make sure to cool the sheets completely before placing more dough on them. Dough will soften and begin to spread on a hot baking sheet.

cooling

- Most cakes can be removed from the pan after 10 to 15 minutes of cooling on a wire rack. Two important exceptions are angel food cakes and flourless cakes. Because they have a more delicate structure, they are cooled in the pan.

- Angel food cakes and some chiffon cakes are cooled in the pan upside down. An angel food cake pan has three metal feet on which the inverted pan stands for cooling. If you are using a tube pan instead of an angel food pan, invert the tube pan over a funnel or narrow-necked bottle for cooling.

- Before attempting to remove a cake from its pan, carefully run a table knife or narrow metal spatula around the outside of the cake to loosen it from the pan. Using oven mitts or hot pads (if the pan is still hot), place a wire cooling rack on top of the cake and pan. Turn the cake over so that the wire rack is on the bottom. Gently shake the cake to release it from the pan. Place the rack on a counter and remove the pan.

- If a cake has cooled too long and will not come out of the pan easily, warm it in a 350°F over for about 5 minutes. Carefully remove it from the pan and let it cool completely on a wire rack.

- Many cookies should be removed from the cookie sheets immediately after baking and placed in a single layer on wire racks to cool.

- Fragile cookies may need to cool slightly on the cookie sheet before being removed to wire racks to cool completely.

- Bar cookies can be cooled and stored in the baking pan.

storing

- Store one-layer cakes in their baking pans, tightly covered.

- Store two- or three-layer cakes in a cake-saver or under a large inverted bowl. If the cake has a fluffy or cooked frosting, insert a teaspoon handle under the edge of the cover to prevent an airtight seal and moisture buildup.

- Cakes with whipped cream frostings or cream fillings should be stored in the refrigerator.

- Store soft and crisp cookies separately at room temperature to prevent changes in texture and flavor.

- Keep soft cookies in airtight containers. If they begin to dry out, add a piece of apple or bread to the container to help them retain moisture.

- Store crisp cookies in containers with loose-fitting lids to prevent moisture build-up. If they become soggy, heat undecorated cookies in a 300°F oven for 3 to 5 minutes to restore crispness.

- Store cookies with sticky glazes, fragile decorations and icings in single layers between sheets of waxed paper.

- Bar cookies can be stored in their own baking pan, covered with aluminum foil or plastic wrap when cool.

freezing

- Unfrosted cakes can be frozen for up to 4 months if wrapped tightly in plastic wrap.

- Frosted cakes should be frozen unwrapped until the frosting hardens, then they can be wrapped tightly in plastic wrap. They can be frozen for up to 2 months.

- Thaw unfrosted cakes in their wrappers at room temperature. For frosted cakes, remove the wrapping and thaw at room temperature or in the refrigerator.

- Cakes with fruit or custard fillings generally do not freeze well because they become soggy when thawed.

- As a rule, crisp cookies freeze better than soft, moist cookies. Rich, buttery bar cookies and brownies are an exception to this rule since they freeze extremely well.

- Freeze baked cookies in airtight containers or freezer bags for up to six months.

- Thaw cookies unwrapped at room temperature.

- Meringue-based cookies do not freeze well, and chocolate-dipped cookies will discolor if frozen.

frosting cakes

- Make sure the cake is completely cool before frosting it.

- Trim the cake, if necessary, before frosting. Then brush off any loose crumbs from the cake's surface with a soft pastry brush.

- To achieve a more professional look, first apply a thin layer of frosting on the cake as a base coat to help seal in any crumbs.

- For the best results, use a flat metal spatula for applying frosting.

- Cake-mix cakes can be slightly more difficult to frost and decorate than cakes made from scratch because they are more tender and crumbly. Placing a cooled cake in the freezer for 30 to 45 minutes will make it easier to frost and decorate.

- Place the cake on a serving plate or covered cake board before frosting it. To keep the plate or board clean, simply tuck strips of waxed paper under the edges of the cake, then frost. When you are finished decorating, gently slide the waxed paper out from under the cake. Then add any final decorations around the base of the cake.

Trimming Cakes

If the tops of the cake layers are rounded, trimming them gives more professional results. Use a serrated knife long enough to cut across  the top in one stroke, such as a bread knife. Use a gentle sawing motion as you cut through the cake.

 The sides of square or rectangular cakes should also be trimmed to make them more even.

If making layers, cut the cake horizontally in half. First remove the cake from the pan and place it on a flat surface. Measure the height of the

cake with a ruler and at the halfway point mark a cutting line with toothpicks. Cut through the cake with a long serrated knife, just above the toothpicks.

Cutting Cakes for Cut-Apart Cakes

For cleaner cutting lines and fewer crumbs, freeze the cake for 30 to 45 minutes. When cutting each cake design, use the diagrams and photos as guides and follow the directions carefully. Toothpicks and  a ruler are helpful to mark designs and act as guidelines while cutting.

Carefully position all of the pieces on a plate, tray or covered cake board. Connect the pieces with some of the frosting. Brush away any crumbs with a soft pastry brush.

Frosting Consistency

The consistency of the frosting is important. Frosting that is too soft will not hold its shape. If the frosting is too soft because the kitchen is warm, refrigerate the frosting for about 15 minutes and keep it chilled while you work. If the frosting is soft because too much liquid was used, beat in some additional sifted powdered sugar. If the frosting is too stiff to spread easily, beat in additional milk, one teaspoon at a time, until the desired consistency is achieved. Commercially prepared canned frosting can also be used.

When piping frosting, it is essential that the frosting be just the right consistency. If it is too soft, the design won't hold fine details. If it is too stiff, it will be very difficult to pipe and some parts of the design may break off. To test for the proper piping consistency, draw a metal spatula through the frosting. It should hold the cut, yet yield to gentle pressure if you poke your finger into the frosting.

To get bright colors and to keep the frosting at the proper consistency, tint frosting with paste food colors. Add a small amount of the paste color with a toothpick, then stir well. Slowly add more color until the frosting is the desired shade. If you use liquid or gel food colors and the frosting becomes too thin, add additional powdered sugar and beat until the desired consistency is reached.

Filling and Frosting Cakes

Place the bottom cake layer on a flat plate and place waxed paper strips under the cake's edge.

Spoon a mound of frosting, about ½ cup, on top of this layer and spread it evenly over the cake with a metal spatula.

Top with a second cake layer. Spread a thin layer of frosting over the entire cake to seal in crumbs; let the cake stand for at least 15 minutes. Then, spread the side with a thicker final layer of frosting,

working from the bottom toward the top and turning the cake as needed. Keep the spatula well coated with frosting so that it doesn't pick up crumbs from the cake. If the spatula does pick up crumbs, wipe it with paper towels before dipping it back into the frosting.

To frost the cake top, spoon a mound of frosting in the center and spread it outward to all edges. Be careful not to mix crumbs into the frosting.

Before decorating the cake, carefully smooth the frosting. Hold a metal spatula under hot running water, shake off the excess water and use the damp spatula to quickly smooth a section of frosting with long strokes in one direction. Repeat dampening and smoothing until the frosting is smooth on the cake top and side.

special decorating equipment

Decorating a cake can be as simple as sprinkling colored sugar over the cake or as elaborate as creating a

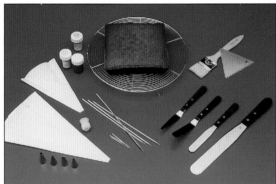

piped design. Of course, the equipment needed varies with the complexity of the cake. The right equipment not only makes cake decorating easier, but also gives more professional results. All of the equipment mentioned here is available in stores that carry cake decorating supplies.

Cake Boards

Some cakes are too large or oddly shaped for standard plates and platters. Use cake boards, cutting boards, cookie sheets or other large flat surfaces. **Cake boards** are made of sturdy cardboard and are available in round or rectangular shapes of various sizes. They can usually be found in craft and kitchenware stores. Cake boards can be covered with foil, greaseproof paper, paper doilies or plastic wrap. To cover, cut the foil or paper 1 to 2 inches larger than the board. Center the board on the reverse side of the paper. Cut slashes in the paper almost to the board along any curved edges. Fold the edges over the board and tape into place. If a cake is very heavy, stack two cake boards together for additional support before covering.

Coupler

A coupler is used to attach tips to the decorating bag and allows you to change tips without removing the frosting from the bag. To use, unscrew the ring. Insert the cone-shaped piece into the narrow end of an empty decorating bag until the narrow end extends slightly beyond the end of the bag (snip off the end of the decorating bag if necessary). Place the coupler ring over the decorating tip. Screw the ring on to hold the tip in place. To change tips, unscrew the ring, remove the tip, replace with the new tip and screw the ring back in place.

Decorating Bags

Decorating bags (also called pastry bags) are cone-shaped bags made of canvas, plastic or plastic-lined cloth and are used to pipe foods, such as frosting and whipped cream, in a decorative pattern. A decorating bag is open at both ends. The smaller opening is usually fitted with a decorative tip. The food to be piped is placed in the larger opening. Some decorating bags are reusable, others are disposable; both types are available in a variety of sizes.

Decorating Tips

These small metal cones are placed at the small opening of a decorating bag. The small end of a decorating tip is formed into a specific shape which makes the food piped through it come out in a particular shape. Decorating tips are available in hundreds of sizes and shapes. They can be categorized by their uses, such as a writing tip or a star tip. Some of the more commonly used tips are as follows: writing tips (numbers 2, 3 and 4), round tips (numbers 5, 7, 8 and 9), open star tips (numbers 13, 14, 15, 16, 18, 22 and 32), closed star tips (numbers 30 and 31), leaf tips (numbers 352 and 67) and drop flower tips (numbers 106, 190 and 225).

Metal Spatulas

Metal spatulas are tools with narrow thin metal blades attached to plastic or wooden handles. They are ideal for spreading. Some are long and rigid whereas others are shorter and flexible. A flat spatula forms a straight line from the handle to the blade. An offset spatula is angled near the handle, causing the handle to be raised slightly. Both types are available in a variety of sizes. A large flexible metal spatula makes smoothing the frosting over large flat areas easier. Use one with a narrow tip to get into small areas.

piping

For each of the following piping techniques, you'll need a decorating bag fitted with the appropriate tip and filled with frosting. If you will be using different tips when decorating, a coupler will make changing tips much easier.

To fill a decorating bag, insert the decorating tip or attach the tip with a coupler.

Fold the top of the bag down and place the frosting in the bag. In general, fill the bag half to two-thirds full, then unfold the top of the bag. Do not fill the bag too full. (If you only need a small amount of frosting, use at least ¼ cup to get enough frosting for piping.)

To prevent the frosting from squeezing out the top of the bag, twist the top tightly against the frosting. Place the twisted end of the bag in the palm of your writing hand with fingers positioned near the bag opening. Place your other hand under the bag to guide the tip.

When piping, hold the bag so the tip is at the angle indicated for the technique. Then, gently squeeze the bag from the top, using even pressure while guiding the tip with your other hand. Squeeze mainly with the palm of your hand rather than your fingers. Be careful not to loosen your grip on the twisted end or the frosting will begin to push up and out of the top of the bag. The size of the decorations you pipe depends on how hard you squeeze as well as on the size of the opening in the tip.

Line (use a writing or small open star tip): Hold the bag so the tip is at a 45° angle to the right. While gently squeezing the bag, guide the tip opening just above the cake in a curved, zigzag, squiggly or straight line. To end the line, stop squeezing, then lift the tip straight up.

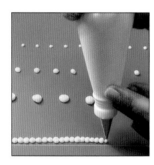

Writing (use a writing tip): Hold the bag so the tip is at a 45° angle to the right for horizontal lines and toward you for vertical lines. While gently squeezing the bag, guide the tip opening just above the cake to form print or script letters. Stop squeezing, then lift the tip at the end of each letter for print letters and at the end of each word for script writing.

Dot (use a round tip): Hold the bag so the tip is at a 90° angle. Position the opening just above the cake and gently squeeze. Lift slightly while still squeezing. When the dot is of the desired size, stop squeezing, then lift the tip straight up. To pipe a dot border, position the tip almost touching the first dot and pipe another dot. Repeat to complete the border.

Star (use an open or closed star tip): Hold the bag so the tip is at a 90° angle. Position the opening just above the cake and gently squeeze. Lift slightly while still squeezing. When the star is of the desired size, stop squeezing, then lift the tip straight up. To pipe a star border, position the tip almost touching the first star and pipe another star. Repeat to complete the border.

Shell (use a round tip, or an open or closed star tip): Hold the bag so the tip is at a 45° angle to the right just above the cake. Squeeze until a small mound is formed for the base of the shell, lifting slightly. Continue squeezing with lighter pressure while pulling the tip away from the base to the right until the tail is of the desired length. Stop squeezing, then lift the tip straight up. To pipe a shell border, position the tip almost touching the tail of the first shell and pipe another shell. Repeat to complete the border. For a double shell border, pipe a shell border as directed. Pipe a second row

of shells offset of the first row so the bases of these shells fill in the tails of the shells in the first row.

Drop Flower (use a drop flower and writing tips): Hold the bag so the tip is at a 90° angle. Position the opening just above the cake and gently squeeze. Lift slightly while still squeezing. When the drop flower is of the desired size, stop squeezing, then lift the tip straight up. Pipe a dot in the

center of each drop flower, using a writing tip. The frosting consistency for drop flowers should be slightly stiffer than for other piping techniques.

Leaf (use a leaf tip): Hold the bag so the tip is at a 45° angle to the right. If using

a number 352 tip (above), position the notch perpendicular to the cake. If using a number 67 tip (below), position the flat part of the tip parallel to the cake. Position the opening just above the cake and gently squeeze until the base of

the leaf builds up slightly. Continue squeezing while pulling the tip out away from the base. When the leaf is of the desired length, stop squeezing, then lift the tip straight up.

garnishing

Sometimes all it takes is that special finishing touch to make desserts go from drab to dazzling. Here are some great ideas for dressing up your cakes and treats.

Caramel Flower

Place one fresh, soft caramel candy square on a very lightly floured surface. Pressing down firmly, roll the caramel out to a 1-inch square. Roll the flattened caramel into a cone to resemble a flower.

Cherry Flower

Cut a maraschino or candied cherry into six wedges, being careful to leave the bottom ⅓ of the cherry uncut. Gently pull out the cherry wedges to resemble flower petals. Place a tiny piece of candied fruit or peel in the center of the flower.

Chocolate Curls

Melt 7 (1-ounce) squares of chocolate; let cool slightly. Pour the melted chocolate onto a cold baking sheet and spread, about ¼ inch thick, into a 6×4-inch rectangle. Let the chocolate stand in a cool, dry place

until set. (Do not refrigerate.) When the chocolate is just set, use a small metal pancake turner to form the curls. Hold the pancake turner at a 45° angle and scrape the chocolate into a curl. Using a toothpick, transfer the curl to waxed paper. Store in a cool, dry place until ready to use.

Chocolate-Dipped Garnishes

Dip cookies, nuts or fruit halfway into melted chocolate, then place them on waxed paper until the chocolate is set.

Chocolate Drizzle or Chocolate Shapes

For chocolate drizzle, place melted chocolate in a plastic food storage bag. Snip off a tiny piece of one corner and drizzle over the frosted cake or treat.

For chocolate shapes, place a sheet of waxed paper onto an inverted baking sheet. Place melted chocolate in a plastic food storage bag and snip off a tiny piece of one corner. While gently squeezing the bag, guide the opening just above the waxed paper to pipe the chocolate in a steady flow, making a variety of small shapes. Stop squeezing and then lift the bag at the

end of each shape. Create flowers, hearts, lattice shapes or any lacy pattern. Let stand in a cool, dry place

until the chocolate is set. (Do not refrigerate.) When the chocolate is set, gently peel the shapes off the waxed paper using a small metal spatula. Store in a cool, dry place until ready to use.

Chocolate Shavings or Grated Chocolate

Create chocolate shavings by dragging a vegetable peeler across a square of chocolate in short quick strokes.

For grated chocolate, working over a waxed paper-lined cutting board, rub chocolate across the rough surface of a grater, letting the pieces fall onto the waxed paper. The large or small holes of the grater can

be used, depending on the size of the chocolate pieces you want.

Chocolate Triangles

Spread 1 square of melted chocolate into a small rectangle on a waxed paper- or parchment-lined baking sheet. Refrigerate the chocolate just until set, about 15 minutes. With the tip of a knife, make a diagonal score cutting the rectangle into two triangles. Refrigerate until firm; break apart to use.

Citrus Knots

Using a vegetable peeler, remove strips of peel from a lemon, lime or orange. Place the strips on a cutting board. If necessary, scrape the cut sides of the peel with a paring knife to remove any white pith. Cut the strips into 3½×⅛-inch pieces. Tie each piece into a knot.

Citrus Peel Rose

Using a vegetable peeler, remove a long, wide strip of peel from around a lemon, lime or orange, being careful not to remove any of the white pitch. Roll up the strip to form a rose shape. Remove a second strip of peel from the fruit, shorter and narrower than the first. Roll up and place it inside the other strip to form the center of the rose.

Citrus Twist

Diagonally cut a lemon, lime or orange into thin slices. Cut a slit through each slice just to the center. Holding each slice with both hands, twist the ends in opposite directions. Place the slices on a plate or the desired food to secure them.

Powdered Sugar or Cocoa Powder

Place the powdered sugar or cocoa powder in a small strainer and gently shake the strainer over the dessert. For fancier designs on cakes, brownies or bar cookies, place a stencil, doily or strips of paper over the top of the dessert before dusting it with sugar or cocoa. Carefully lift off the stencil, doily or paper strips, holding firmly by the edges and pulling straight up.

Powdered Sugar Glazes

Combine 1 cup of sifted powdered sugar and 5 teaspoons of milk in a small bowl. Add ½ teaspoon of vanilla extract or another flavoring, if desired. Stir until smooth. If the glaze is too thin, add additional powdered sugar; if it is too thick, add additional milk, ½ teaspoon at a time. Use the glaze white or tint it with food coloring to fit any occasion.

Strawberry Fan

Place a strawberry on a cutting board with the pointed end facing you. Make four or five lengthwise cuts from just below the stem end of the strawberry the pointed end. Fan the slices apart slightly, being careful to keep all of the slices attached to the cap.

Sugars, Sprinkles or Candies

Sprinkle cookies with coarse sugar, colored sugars or sprinkles before baking. Or, after baking, cakes and cookies can be frosted and then topped with colored sugar, sprinkles or candies. To decorate a cake, coat the side with sprinkles while the frosting is still soft.

Toasted Coconut or Nuts

Spread coconut or nuts in a thin layer on an ungreased baking sheet. Bake in a preheated 325°F oven 7 to 10 minutes or until golden, stirring occasionally to promote even browning and prevent burning. Allow coconut and nuts to cool before using. Toasted nuts will darken and become crisper as they cool. To decorate a cake, sprinkle the side with the toasted coconut or nuts while the frosting is still soft.

Tinted Coconut

Place ½ teaspoon of milk or water in a medium bowl. Add a few drops of liquid food coloring; stir until well blended. Add 1 to 1⅓ cups flaked coconut and toss with a fork until the coconut is evenly tinted. Add more diluted food coloring, if necessary, until the desired shade is reached. To decorate a cake, sprinkle the side with the tinted coconut while the frosting is still soft.

melting chocolate

Be sure the utensils you use for melting chocolate are completely dry. Moisture causes chocolate to become stiff and grainy. If this happens, add ½ teaspoon of shortening (not butter) for each ounce of chocolate and stir until smooth. Chocolate scorches easily and cannot be used once it is scorched. Follow one of these three methods for successful melting.

Double Boiler: This is the safest method because it prevents scorching. Place the chocolate in the top of a double boiler or in a bowl over hot, not boiling, water; stir until smooth. (Make sure the water remains just below a simmer and is one inch below the top pan.) Be careful that no steam or water gets into the chocolate.

Direct Heat: Place the chocolate in a heavy saucepan and melt over very low heat, stirring constantly. Remove the chocolate from the heat as soon as it is melted. Be sure to watch the chocolate carefully since it is easily scorched with this method.

Microwave Oven: Place 4 to 6 unwrapped 1-ounce squares of chocolate or 1 cup of chocolate chips in a small microwavable bowl. Microwave at High (100% power) for 1 to 1½ minutes. Stir after 1 minute and at 30-second intervals after the first minute. Be sure to stir microwaved chocolate since it can retain its original shape even when melted.

serving

Bar Cookies: For a fancy appearance, try cutting bar cookies into triangles or diamonds. For triangles, simply cut the bars into squares or rectangles and then cut them in half into triangles. For diamonds, first cut straight lines 1 or 1½ inches apart the length of the baking pan, then cut straight lines 1½ inches apart diagonally across the pan.

Cookies: For a festive way to serve cookies, line a basket, box or tin with a colorful napkin or tissue paper. Place the cookies in the container in neat rows or pile them up high.

Cakes: For a pretty presentation, drizzle 1 to 2 tablespoons of your favorite flavor of ice cream topping over individual serving plates before placing the cake slice on it. For a feathered sauce, spoon the desired sauce onto individual serving plates. Tilt the plates to spread the sauce evenly. Use a spoon or decorating bag fitted with a writing tip to drizzle a contrasting sauce in a spiral design over the first sauce. Feather by drawing a narrow metal spatula or knife through the lines at regular intervals.

classic
cakes

Creamy Coconut Cake with Almond Filling

1 package (about 18 ounces) white cake mix
1 cup sour cream
3 eggs
½ cup vegetable oil
1 teaspoon vanilla
1 teaspoon coconut extract
1 can (12½ ounces) almond filling
2 containers (16 ounces each) creamy coconut frosting
½ cup sliced almonds

1. Preheat oven to 350°F. Grease and flour two 9-inch round baking pans.

2. Combine cake mix, sour cream, eggs, oil, vanilla and coconut extract in large bowl. Beat with electric mixer at low speed 3 minutes or until well blended. Divide evenly between prepared pans. Bake 30 to 35 minutes or until toothpicks inserted into centers come out clean. Cool completely in pans on wire racks.

3. Remove cakes from pans. Slice each cake horizontally in half to make 4 layers. Place one cake layer on serving plate; spread with half of almond filling. Top with second cake layer; spread with ½ cup coconut frosting. Top with third cake layer; spread with remaining almond filling. Top with fourth cake layer; spread remaining coconut frosting over top and side of cake. Sprinkle with almonds.

Makes 8 to 12 servings

Creamy Coconut Cake with Almond Filling

Fudge Cake with Melba Topping

Cake
   **1 package DUNCAN HINES® Moist Deluxe® Dark Chocolate Fudge
      Cake Mix**
   Egg substitute product equal to 3 eggs
 1¼ cups water
   ½ cup vegetable oil

Melba Topping
   **1 package (12 ounces) frozen dry pack raspberries, thawed,
      drained and juice reserved**
   ½ cup sugar
   2 teaspoons cornstarch
   ½ teaspoon grated lemon peel
   1 can (29 ounces) sliced peaches in lite syrup, drained

1. Preheat oven to 350°F. Grease and flour 13×9×2-inch baking pan.

2. For cake, combine cake mix, egg substitute, water and oil in large bowl. Beat at medium speed with electric mixer for 2 minutes. Pour into prepared pan. Bake at 350°F for 35 to 40 minutes or until toothpick inserted in center comes out clean. Cool completely.

3. For topping, combine reserved raspberry juice, sugar, cornstarch and lemon peel in medium saucepan. Bring to a boil. Reduce heat and cook until thickened, stirring constantly. Stir in raspberries. Cool.

4. Cut cake into serving squares. Place several peach slices on top of cake square. Spoon raspberry sauce over peaches and cake. Serve immediately.

Makes 20 servings

Hint: To separate juice from raspberries in one step, allow berries to thaw at room temperature in a strainer placed over a bowl.

Fudge Cake with Melba Topping

Angel Food Roll with Strawberry Sauce

1 package (16 ounces) angel food cake mix, plus ingredients to prepare mix
¼ cup plus 2 tablespoons powdered sugar, divided
1 quart strawberry low-fat frozen yogurt
1 container (10 ounces) frozen sliced strawberries with sugar, thawed
1 tablespoon lemon juice
1½ teaspoons cornstarch

1. Preheat oven to 350°F. Line bottom of 15×10-inch jelly-roll pan with waxed paper. Prepare cake mix according to package directions; pour evenly into prepared pan. Bake about 20 minutes or until cake is golden brown and springs back when lightly touched. Cool on wire rack 15 minutes.

2. Place clean kitchen towel on flat surface. Sift ¼ cup powdered sugar over towel; invert cake on top of sugar. Carefully peel off waxed paper. Starting at short end, roll cake up with towel, jelly-roll style. Cool 30 minutes, seam side down, on wire rack.

3. Remove frozen yogurt from freezer to soften slightly. Carefully unroll cake. Place pieces of frozen yogurt on top of cake; spread to edges. Reroll filled cake; cover tightly with plastic wrap. Freeze at least 3 hours or overnight.

4. To prepare strawberry sauce, combine strawberries, lemon juice and cornstarch in small saucepan; bring to a boil over medium heat. Reduce heat to low; cook and stir 2 to 3 minutes or until sauce has thickened. Cool; refrigerate until ready to serve.

5. To complete recipe, remove cake from freezer 15 minutes before serving. Dust with remaining 2 tablespoons powdered sugar. Cut into slices with serrated knife; serve with strawberry sauce. *Makes 8 servings*

Make-Ahead Time: at least 3 hours or up to 24 hours before serving
Final Prep Time: 20 minutes

Angel Food Roll with Strawberry Sauce

Butterscotch Bundt Cake

1 package (18¼ ounces) yellow cake mix
1 package (4-serving size) butterscotch-flavored instant pudding mix
1 cup water
3 eggs
2 teaspoons ground cinnamon
½ cup chopped pecans
   Powdered sugar (optional)

Preheat oven to 325°F. Spray 10-inch Bundt pan with nonstick cooking spray. Combine all ingredients except pecans and powdered sugar in large bowl. Beat with electric mixer at medium-high speed 2 minutes or until blended. Stir in pecans. Pour into prepared pan. Bake 40 to 50 minutes or until cake springs back when lightly touched. Cool on wire rack 10 minutes. Invert cake onto serving plate. Cool completely. Sprinkle with powdered sugar, if desired.   *Makes 12 to 16 servings*

Sour Cream Cherry Cake

1 (9-ounce) package yellow cake mix
1 egg
1½ cups reduced-fat (2%) milk, divided
1 (3½-ounce) package vanilla pudding mix
½ cup dairy sour cream
½ teaspoon grated lemon peel
2 cups pitted Northwest fresh sweet cherries
2 tablespoons currant jelly, melted
   Mint sprigs
1 cup sweetened whipped cream (optional)

Prepare yellow cake according to package directions using egg and ½ cup milk. Pour batter into flan pan and bake according to package directions. Prepare vanilla pudding according to package directions using remaining 1 cup milk; remove from heat and stir in sour cream and lemon peel. When cake is cool, fill with vanilla pudding. Top with cherries; brush with melted jelly. Garnish with mint. Serve with whipped cream, if desired.   *Makes 8 servings*

*Favorite recipe from **Northwest Cherry Growers***

Butterscotch Bundt Cake

Chocolate Banana Cake

Cake
>**1 package DUNCAN HINES® Moist Deluxe® Devil's Food Cake Mix**
>**3 eggs**

1⅓ cups milk
>**½ cup vegetable oil**

Topping
>**1 package (4-serving size) banana cream instant pudding and pie filling mix**

1 cup milk
1 cup whipping cream, whipped
1 medium banana
>**Lemon juice**
>**Chocolate sprinkles for garnish**

1. Preheat oven to 350°F. Grease and flour 13×9×2-inch pan.

2. For cake, combine cake mix, eggs, milk and oil in large bowl. Beat at low speed with electric mixer until moistened. Beat at medium speed 2 minutes. Pour into pan. Bake at 350°F for 35 to 38 minutes or until toothpick inserted in center comes out clean. Cool completely.

3. For topping, combine pudding mix and milk in large bowl. Stir until smooth. Fold in whipped cream. Spread on top of cooled cake. Slice banana; dip in lemon juice and arrange on top. Garnish with chocolate sprinkles. Refrigerate until ready to serve.

Makes 12 to 16 servings

Hint: A wire whisk is a great utensil to use when making instant pudding. It quickly eliminates all lumps.

Chocolate Banana Cake

Dump Cake

1 can (20 ounces) crushed pineapple with juice, undrained
1 can (21 ounces) cherry pie filling
1 package DUNCAN HINES® Moist Deluxe® Yellow Cake Mix
1 cup chopped pecans or walnuts
½ cup butter or margarine, cut into thin slices

1. Preheat oven to 350°F. Grease 13×9-inch pan.

2. Dump pineapple with juice into prepared pan. Spread evenly. Dump in pie filling. Spread evenly. Sprinkle cake mix evenly over cherry layer. Sprinkle pecans over cake mix. Dot with butter. Bake at 350°F for 50 minutes or until top is lightly browned. Serve warm or at room temperature.   *Makes 12 to 16 servings*

Note: You can use Duncan Hines® Moist Deluxe® Pineapple Supreme Cake Mix in place of Moist Deluxe® Yellow Cake Mix.

Pumpkin Crunch Cake

1 package (18.25 ounces) yellow cake mix, *divided*
1⅔ cups LIBBY'S® Easy Pumpkin Pie Mix
2 eggs
2 teaspoons pumpkin pie spice
⅓ cup flaked coconut
¼ cup chopped nuts
3 tablespoons butter or margarine, softened

PREHEAT oven to 350°F. Grease 13×9-inch baking pan.

COMBINE *3 cups* yellow cake mix, pumpkin pie mix, eggs and pumpkin pie spice in large mixer bowl. Beat on medium speed of electric mixer for 2 minutes. Pour into prepared baking pan.

COMBINE *remaining* cake mix, coconut and nuts in small bowl; cut in butter with pastry blender or two knives until mixture is crumbly. Sprinkle over batter.

BAKE for 30 to 35 minutes or until wooden pick inserted in center comes out clean. Cool in pan on wire rack.   *Makes 20 servings*

Dump Cake

Banana Fudge Layer Cake

1 package DUNCAN HINES® Moist Deluxe® Yellow Cake Mix
1 ⅓ cups water
3 eggs
⅓ cup vegetable oil
1 cup mashed ripe bananas (about 3 medium)
1 container DUNCAN HINES® Chocolate Frosting

1. Preheat oven to 350°F. Grease and flour two 9-inch round cake pans.

2. Combine cake mix, water, eggs and oil in large bowl. Beat at low speed with electric mixer until moistened. Beat at medium speed 2 minutes. Stir in bananas.

3. Pour into prepared pans. Bake at 350°F for 28 to 31 minutes or until toothpick inserted in center comes out clean. Cool in pans 15 minutes. Remove from pans; cool completely.

4. Fill and frost cake with frosting. Garnish as desired.

Makes 12 to 16 servings

Cran-Lemon Coffee Cake

1 package (about 18 ounces) yellow pudding-in-the-mix cake mix
1 cup water
3 eggs
⅓ cup butter, melted and cooled
¼ cup fresh lemon juice
1 tablespoon grated lemon peel
1 ½ cups coarsely chopped cranberries

1. Preheat oven to 350°F. Grease and flour 12-inch tube pan. Beat cake mix, water, eggs, butter, lemon juice and lemon peel in large bowl with electric mixer at low speed 2 minutes. Fold in cranberries. Spread batter evenly in prepared pan.

2. Bake about 55 minutes or until toothpick inserted 1 inch from edge comes out clean. Cool in pan on wire rack 10 minutes. Remove from pan; cool on wire rack. Serve warm or at room temperature.

Makes 12 servings

Banana Fudge Layer Cake

Spicy Apple Upside Down Cake

Cake
- ½ **cup (1 stick) butter, melted**
- ¾ **cup packed dark brown sugar**
- 2 **Braeburn apples, thinly sliced**
- 1 **package (about 18 ounces) carrot cake mix, plus ingredients to prepare mix**

Sauce
- ½ **cup (1 stick) butter**
- ½ **cup packed dark brown sugar**
- ¼ **cup whiskey**

1. Preheat oven to 350°F. Lightly grease 9-inch springform pan. Wrap outside of pan tightly in heavy-duty aluminum foil.

2. For cake, pour melted butter into pan; tilt pan to spread butter evenly over bottom of pan. Sprinkle brown sugar evenly over butter. Arrange apple slices, overlapping slightly, in spiral pattern in pan.

3. Prepare cake mix according to package directions. Carefully spoon cake batter over apples. Bake 1 hour or until toothpick inserted into center comes out clean.

4. Immediately invert cake onto serving plate; let stand without removing pan about 5 minutes. Remove side and bottom of pan; let cool completely.

5. For sauce, combine butter and brown sugar in small microwavable bowl; cover with plastic wrap. Microwave at HIGH 1 minute. Stir; microwave 30 seconds or until melted and well blended. Stir whiskey into butter mixture.

6. Starting at outer edges of cake, spoon whiskey sauce over entire cake, allowing sauce to run down side. *Makes 12 servings*

Spicy Apple Upside Down Cake

Fudge Ribbon Cake

1 (18¼-ounce) package chocolate cake mix, plus ingredients to prepare mix
1 (8-ounce) package cream cheese, softened
2 tablespoons butter or margarine, softened
1 tablespoon cornstarch
1 (14-ounce) can EAGLE BRAND® Sweetened Condensed Milk (NOT evaporated milk)
1 egg
1 teaspoon vanilla extract
Chocolate Glaze (recipe follows)

1. Preheat oven to 350°F. Grease and flour 13×9-inch baking pan. Prepare cake mix as package directs. Pour batter into prepared pan.

2. In small mixing bowl, beat cream cheese, butter and cornstarch until fluffy. Gradually beat in Eagle Brand. Add egg and vanilla; beat until smooth. Spoon evenly over cake batter.

3. Bake 40 minutes or until wooden pick inserted near center comes out clean. Cool. Prepare Chocolate Glaze and drizzle over cake. Store covered in refrigerator.

Makes 10 to 12 servings

Chocolate Glaze: In small saucepan over low heat, melt 1 (1-ounce) square unsweetened or semi-sweet chocolate and 1 tablespoon butter or margarine with 2 tablespoons water. Remove from heat. Stir in ¾ cup powdered sugar and ½ teaspoon vanilla extract. Stir until smooth and well blended. Makes about ⅓ cup.

Prep Time: 20 minutes
Bake Time: 40 minutes

Fudge Ribbon Cake

Orange Glow Bundt Cake

**1 (18.25-ounce) package moist yellow cake mix, plus ingredients to
    prepare mix**
1 tablespoon grated orange peel
1 cup orange juice
¼ cup sugar
1 tablespoon TABASCO® brand Pepper Sauce
1¾ cups confectioners' sugar

Preheat oven to 375°F. Grease 12-cup Bundt pan. Prepare cake mix according to
package directions, adding orange peel to batter. Bake 35 to 40 minutes or until
toothpick inserted in center of cake comes out clean.

Meanwhile, heat orange juice, sugar and TABASCO® Sauce to boiling in 1-quart
saucepan. Reduce heat to low; simmer, uncovered, 5 minutes. Remove from heat.
Reserve ¼ cup orange juice mixture for glaze.

Remove cake from oven. With wooden skewer, poke holes in cake (in pan) in several
places. Spoon remaining orange juice mixture over cake. Cool cake in pan 10 minutes.
Carefully invert cake onto wire rack to cool completely.

Combine reserved ¼ cup orange juice mixture and confectioners' sugar in small bowl
until smooth. Place cake on platter; spoon glaze over cake. Garnish with mint leaves
and orange slices, if desired.   *Makes 12 servings*

tip

When grating orange peel, grate only the outer
orange layer of the skin, which is very sweet and
flavorful. Avoid grating into the white pith, as it has
a bitter taste.

Orange Glow Bundt Cake

Aunt Ruth's Favorite White Cake

> **1 package (18¼ ounces) white cake mix**
> **1¼ cups water**
> **3 eggs**
> **2 tablespoons vegetable oil**
> **1 teaspoon vanilla**
> **½ teaspoon almond extract**
> **Creamy White Frosting (recipe follows)**

1. Preheat oven to 350°F. Grease and flour two 8- or 9-inch round cake pans.

2. Combine cake mix, water, eggs and oil in large bowl. Beat at medium speed of electric mixer until well blended. Add vanilla and almond extract; mix until well blended. Divide batter evenly between prepared pans.

3. Bake 30 to 35 minutes or until toothpicks inserted into centers come out clean. Cool in pans on wire racks 10 minutes. Remove cakes from pans; cool completely on wire racks.

4. Prepare Creamy White Frosting. Fill and frost cake with frosting.

Makes one 2-layer cake

Creamy White Frosting

> **1 cup milk**
> **3 tablespoons all-purpose flour**
> **1 cup (2 sticks) butter, softened**
> **1 cup powdered sugar**
> **1 teaspoon vanilla**

1. Combine milk and flour in medium saucepan; cook and stir over low heat until thickened. Cool.

2. Beat butter in large bowl until creamy. Add powdered sugar; beat until fluffy. Blend in vanilla. Add flour mixture; beat until thick and smooth.

Aunt Ruth's Favorite White Cake

Spice Cake with Fresh Peach Sauce

Cake
> **1 package DUNCAN HINES® Moist Deluxe® Spice Cake Mix**
> **3 egg whites**

1¼ cups water
> **⅓ cup vegetable oil**
> **Confectioners' sugar (optional)**

Sauce
> **6 cups sliced fresh peaches**
> **1 cup water**
> **⅓ cup sugar**
> **⅛ teaspoon ground cinnamon**

1. Preheat oven to 350°F. Grease and flour 10-inch Bundt or tube pan.

2. For cake, place cake mix, egg whites, water and oil in large bowl. Beat at low speed with electric mixer until blended. Beat at medium speed 2 minutes. Pour into prepared pan. Bake at 350°F for 42 to 47 minutes or until toothpick inserted near center comes out clean. Cool in pan 25 minutes. Invert onto serving plate. Cool completely. Dust with confectioners' sugar, if desired.

3. For sauce, combine peaches and water in large saucepan. Cook over medium heat 5 minutes. Reduce heat to low. Cover and simmer 10 minutes. Cool. Reserve ½ cup peach slices. Combine remaining peaches and any cooking liquid, sugar and cinnamon in blender or food processor. Process until smooth. Stir in reserved peach slices. To serve, spoon peach sauce over cake slices. *Makes 12 to 16 servings*

Note: Use ¾ cup egg substitute in place of egg whites, if desired.

Hint: The fresh peach sauce can be served either warm or chilled.

Spice Cake with Fresh Peach Sauce

Rich Caramel Cake

1 (14-ounce) package caramels, unwrapped
½ cup (1 stick) butter or margarine
1 (14-ounce) can EAGLE BRAND® Sweetened Condensed Milk
   (NOT evaporated milk)
1 (18.25- or 18.5-ounce) package chocolate cake mix, plus
   ingredients to prepare mix
1 cup coarsely chopped pecans

1. Preheat oven to 350°F. In heavy saucepan over low heat, melt caramels and butter. Remove from heat; add Eagle Brand. Mix well. Set aside caramel mixture. Prepare cake mix as package directs.

2. Spread 2 cups cake batter into greased 13×9-inch baking pan; bake 15 minutes. Spread caramel mixture evenly over cake; spread remaining cake batter over caramel mixture. Top with pecans. Return to oven; bake 30 to 35 minutes or until cake springs back when lightly touched. Cool.   *Makes 10 to 12 servings*

Upside-Down German Chocolate Cake

1½ cups flaked coconut
1½ cups chopped pecans
   1 package DUNCAN HINES® Moist Deluxe® German Chocolate or
      Classic Chocolate Cake Mix
   1 package (8 ounces) cream cheese, softened
½ cup butter or margarine, melted
   1 pound (3½ to 4 cups) confectioners' sugar

1. Preheat oven to 350°F. Grease and flour 13×9-inch pan.

2. Spread coconut evenly on bottom of prepared pan. Sprinkle with pecans. Prepare cake mix as directed on package. Pour over coconut and pecans. Combine cream cheese and melted butter in medium mixing bowl. Beat at low speed with electric mixer until creamy. Add sugar; beat until blended and smooth. Drop by spoonfuls evenly over cake batter. Bake at 350°F for 45 to 50 minutes or until toothpick inserted halfway to bottom of cake comes out clean. Cool completely in pan. To serve, cut into individual pieces; turn upside down onto plate.   *Makes 12 to 16 servings*

Rich Caramel Cake

Strawberry Stripe Refrigerator Cake

Cake
> **1 package DUNCAN HINES® Moist Deluxe® Classic White Cake Mix**
> **2 packages (10 ounces) frozen sweetened strawberry slices, thawed**

Topping
> **1 package (4-serving size) vanilla-flavor instant pudding and pie filling mix**
> **1 cup milk**
> **1 cup whipping cream, whipped**
> **Fresh strawberries for garnish (optional)**

1. Preheat oven to 350°F. Grease and flour 13×9×2-inch pan.

2. For cake, prepare, bake and cool following package directions. Poke holes 1 inch apart in top of cake using handle of wooden spoon. Purée thawed strawberries with juice in blender or food processor. Spoon evenly over top of cake, allowing mixture to soak into holes.

3. For topping, combine pudding mix and milk in large bowl. Stir until smooth. Fold in whipped cream. Spread over cake. Decorate with fresh strawberries, if desired. Refrigerate at least 4 hours. *Makes 12 to 16 servings*

Variation: For a Neapolitan Refrigerator Cake, substitute Duncan Hines® Moist Deluxe® Devil's Food Cake Mix for White Cake Mix and follow directions listed above.

Strawberry Stripe Refrigerator Cake

Banana-Coconut Crunch Cake

Cake
    1 package DUNCAN HINES® Moist Deluxe® Banana Supreme Cake Mix
    1 package (4-serving size) banana-flavor instant pudding and pie filling mix
    1 can (16 ounces) fruit cocktail in juice, undrained
    4 eggs
    ¼ cup vegetable oil
    1 cup flaked coconut
    ½ cup chopped pecans
    ½ cup firmly packed brown sugar

Glaze
    ¾ cup granulated sugar
    ½ cup butter or margarine
    ½ cup evaporated milk
    1⅓ cups flaked coconut

1. Preheat oven to 350°F. Grease and flour 13×9×2-inch pan.

2. For cake, combine cake mix, pudding mix, fruit cocktail with juice, eggs and oil in large bowl. Beat at medium speed with electric mixer for 4 minutes. Stir in 1 cup coconut. Pour into prepared pan. Combine pecans and brown sugar in small bowl. Stir until well mixed. Sprinkle over batter. Bake at 350°F for 45 to 50 minutes or until toothpick inserted in center comes out clean.

3. For glaze, combine granulated sugar, butter and evaporated milk in medium saucepan. Bring to a boil. Cook for 2 minutes, stirring occasionally. Remove from heat. Stir in 1⅓ cups coconut. Pour over warm cake. Serve warm or at room temperature. *Makes 12 to 16 servings*

Banana-Coconut Crunch Cake

Cappuccino Cake

½ cup (3 ounces) semisweet chocolate chips
½ cup chopped hazelnuts, walnuts or pecans
1 (18.25-ounce) package yellow cake mix
¼ cup instant espresso coffee powder
2 teaspoons ground cinnamon
1¼ cups water
3 eggs
⅓ cup FILIPPO BERIO® Pure or Extra Light Tasting Olive Oil
Powdered sugar
1 (15-ounce) container ricotta cheese
2 teaspoons granulated sugar
Additional ground cinnamon

Preheat oven to 325°F. Grease 10-inch (12-cup) Bundt pan or 10-inch tube pan with olive oil. Sprinkle lightly with flour.

In small bowl, combine chocolate chips and hazelnuts. Spoon evenly into bottom of prepared pan.

In large bowl, combine cake mix, coffee powder and 2 teaspoons cinnamon. Add water, eggs and olive oil. Beat with electric mixer at low speed until dry ingredients are moistened. Beat at medium speed 2 minutes. Pour batter over topping in pan.

Bake 60 minutes or until toothpick inserted near center comes out clean. Cool on wire rack 15 minutes. Remove from pan. Place cake, fluted side up, on serving plate. Cool completely. Sprinkle with powdered sugar.

In medium bowl, combine ricotta cheese and granulated sugar. Sprinkle with cinnamon. Serve cheese mixture alongside slices of cake. Serve cake with cappuccino, espresso or your favorite coffee, if desired.   *Makes 12 to 16 servings*

Cappuccino Cake

Refreshing Lemon Cake

**1 package DUNCAN HINES® Moist Deluxe® Butter Recipe Golden
Cake Mix**
**1 container DUNCAN HINES® Creamy Home-Style Cream Cheese
Frosting**
¾ cup purchased lemon curd
Lemon drop candies, crushed for garnish (optional)

1. Preheat oven to 375°F. Grease and flour two 8- or 9-inch round cake pans.

2. Prepare, bake and cool cake following package directions for basic recipe.

3. To assemble, place one cake layer on serving plate. Place ¼ cup Cream Cheese frosting in small resealable plastic bag. Snip off one corner. Pipe a bead of frosting on top of layer around outer edge. Fill remaining area with lemon curd. Top with second cake layer. Spread remaining frosting on side and top of cake. Garnish top of cake with crushed lemon candies, if desired. *Makes 12 to 16 servings*

Note: You can substitute Duncan Hines® Vanilla or Vanilla Buttercream frosting for the Cream Cheese frosting, if desired.

Cherry-Mallow Cake

4 cups miniature marshmallows (about ¾ of 10½-ounce package)
**1 (18.25-ounce) package yellow cake mix, plus ingredients to
prepare mix**
1 (21-ounce) can cherry pie filling

Spray 13×9×2-inch baking pan with vegetable cooking spray. Place marshmallows evenly in bottom of pan.

Prepare cake mix according to package directions. Pour batter over marshmallows. Spoon cherry filling evenly over cake batter.

Bake in preheated 350°F oven 30 to 40 minutes. Top of cake will be bubbly and marshmallows will be sticky. Let cool before serving. *Makes 15 servings*

Favorite recipe from **Cherry Marketing Institute**

Refreshing Lemon Cake

Take-Along Cake

1 package DUNCAN HINES® Moist Deluxe® Swiss Chocolate Cake Mix
1 package (12 ounces) semisweet chocolate chips
1 cup miniature marshmallows
¼ cup butter or margarine, melted
½ cup packed brown sugar
½ cup chopped pecans or walnuts

1. Preheat oven to 350°F. Grease and flour 13×9-inch pan.

2. Prepare cake mix as directed on package. Add chocolate chips and marshmallows to batter. Pour into prepared pan. Drizzle melted butter over batter. Sprinkle with sugar and top with pecans. Bake at 350°F for 45 to 55 minutes or until toothpick inserted in center comes out clean. Serve warm or cool completely in pan.

Makes 12 to 16 servings

Hint: To keep leftover pecans fresh, store them in the freezer in an airtight container.

Blueberry Angel Food Cake Rolls

1 package DUNCAN HINES® Angel Food Cake Mix
¼ cup confectioners' sugar plus additional for dusting
1 can (21 ounces) blueberry pie filling
Mint leaves for garnish (optional)

1. Preheat oven to 350°F. Line two 15½×10½×1-inch jelly-roll pans with aluminum foil.

2. Prepare cake mix as directed on package. Divide and spread evenly into prepared pans. Cut through batter with knife or spatula to remove large air bubbles. Bake at 350°F for 15 minutes or until set. Invert cakes at once onto clean, lint-free dishtowels dusted with confectioners' sugar. Remove foil carefully. Roll up each cake with towel jelly-roll fashion, starting at short end. Cool completely.

3. Unroll cakes. Spread about 1 cup blueberry pie filling to within 1 inch of edges on each cake. Reroll and place seam-side down on serving plate. Dust with ¼ cup confectioners' sugar. Garnish with mint leaves, if desired.

Makes 2 cakes (8 servings each)

Variation: For a change in flavor, substitute cherry pie filling for the blueberry pie filling.

Take-Along Cake

Sock-It-To-Me Cake

Streusel Filling
   1 package DUNCAN HINES® Moist Deluxe® Butter Recipe Golden Cake Mix, divided
   2 tablespoons brown sugar
   2 teaspoons ground cinnamon
   1 cup finely chopped pecans

Cake
   4 eggs
   1 cup dairy sour cream
   ⅓ cup vegetable oil
   ¼ cup granulated sugar
   ¼ cup water

Glaze
   1 cup confectioners' sugar
   1 to 2 tablespoons milk

1. Preheat oven to 375°F. Grease and flour 10-inch tube pan.

2. For streusel filling, combine 2 tablespoons cake mix, brown sugar and cinnamon in medium bowl. Stir in pecans. Set aside.

3. For cake, combine remaining cake mix, eggs, sour cream, oil, granulated sugar and water in large bowl. Beat at medium speed with electric mixer 2 minutes. Pour two-thirds of batter into prepared pan. Sprinkle with streusel filling. Spoon remaining batter evenly over filling. Bake at 375°F for 45 to 55 minutes or until toothpick inserted in center comes out clean. Cool in pan 25 minutes. Invert onto serving plate. Cool completely.

4. For glaze, combine confectioners' sugar and milk in small bowl. Stir until smooth. Drizzle over cake.   *Makes 12 to 16 servings*

Hint: For a quick glaze, place ½ cup Duncan Hines® Creamy Homestyle Vanilla Frosting in small microwave-safe bowl. Microwave at HIGH (100% power) 10 seconds; add 5 to 10 seconds, if needed. Stir until smooth and thin.

Sock-It-To-Me Cake

Chocolate Toffee Cream Cake

1 package DUNCAN HINES® Moist Deluxe® Dark Chocolate Fudge Cake Mix
3 eggs
1⅓ cups water
½ cup vegetable oil
1 package (6 ounces) milk chocolate English toffee bits, divided
1 container (12 ounces) extra creamy non-dairy whipped topping, thawed

1. Preheat oven to 350°F. Grease and flour two 9-inch round cake pans.

2. Blend cake mix, eggs, water and oil in large mixing bowl until moistened. Beat at medium speed with electric mixer for 4 minutes. Pour into prepared pans. Bake at 350°F for 30 to 33 minutes or until toothpick inserted in center comes out clean. Cool in pans 15 minutes. Remove cakes from pans. Cool completely.

3. Reserve ¼ cup toffee bits; fold remaining bits into whipped topping. Place one cake layer on serving plate; spread with ¾ cup topping mixture. Top with remaining layer. Frost side and top with remaining topping mixture; garnish with reserved bits. Refrigerate until ready to serve. *Makes 12 to 16 servings*

Note: If chocolate toffee bits are not available, 4 chocolate covered toffee candy bars can be substituted. Process bars in a food processor until chopped.

tip

Refrigerate eggs immediately after purchasing. To prevent them from absorbing odors from other foods, store them in their original carton.

Chocolate Toffee Cream Cake

Della Robbia Cake

1 package DUNCAN HINES® Angel Food Cake Mix
1½ teaspoons grated lemon peel
1 cup water
6 tablespoons granulated sugar
1½ tablespoons cornstarch
1 tablespoon lemon juice
½ teaspoon vanilla extract
Few drops red food coloring
6 cling peach slices
6 medium strawberries, sliced

1. Preheat oven to 375°F.

2. Prepare cake mix as directed on package, adding lemon peel. Bake and cool cake as directed on package.

3. Combine water, sugar and cornstarch in small saucepan. Cook on medium-high heat until mixture thickens and clears. Remove from heat. Stir in lemon juice, vanilla extract and food coloring.

4. Alternate peach slices with strawberry slices around top of cake. Pour glaze over fruit and top of cake.   *Makes 12 to 16 servings*

Hint: For angel food cakes, always use a totally grease-free cake pan to get the best volume.

Della Robbia Cake

Pineapple Upside-Down Cake

Topping
- ½ **cup butter or margarine**
- 1 **cup firmly packed brown sugar**
- 1 **can (20 ounces) pineapple slices, well drained**
- **Maraschino cherries, drained and halved**
- **Walnut halves**

Cake
- 1 **package DUNCAN HINES® Moist Deluxe® Pineapple Supreme Cake Mix**
- 1 **package (4-serving size) vanilla-flavor instant pudding and pie filling mix**
- 4 **eggs**
- 1 **cup water**
- ½ **cup oil**

1. Preheat oven to 350°F.

2. For topping, melt butter over low heat in 12-inch cast-iron skillet or skillet with oven-proof handle. Remove from heat. Stir in brown sugar. Spread to cover bottom of skillet. Arrange pineapple slices, maraschino cherries and walnut halves in skillet. Set aside.

3. For cake, combine cake mix, pudding mix, eggs, water and oil in large mixing bowl. Beat at medium speed with electric mixer for 2 minutes. Pour batter evenly over fruit in skillet. Bake at 350°F for 1 hour or until toothpick inserted in center comes out clean. Invert onto serving plate.   *Makes 16 to 20 servings*

Note: Cake can be made in a 13×9×2-inch pan. Bake at 350°F for 45 to 55 minutes or until toothpick inserted in center comes out clean. Cake is also delicious using Duncan Hines® Moist Deluxe® Yellow Cake Mix.

Pineapple Upside-Down Cake

just for kids

Berry Surprise Cupcakes

> **1 package DUNCAN HINES® Moist Deluxe® White Cake Mix**
> **3 egg whites**
> **1⅓ cups water**
> **2 tablespoons vegetable oil**
> **3 sheets (0.5 ounce each) strawberry chewy fruit snacks**
> **1 container DUNCAN HINES® Vanilla Frosting**
> **2 pouches (0.9 ounce each) chewy fruit snack shapes, for garnish (optional)**

1. Preheat oven to 350°F. Place paper liners in 24 (2½-inch) muffin cups.

2. Combine cake mix, egg whites, water and oil in large bowl. Beat at low speed with electric mixer until moistened. Beat at medium speed 2 minutes. Fill each liner half full with batter.

3. Cut three fruit snack sheets into 9 equal pieces. (You will have 3 extra squares.) Place each fruit snack piece on top of batter in each cup. Pour remaining batter equally over each. Bake at 350°F for 18 to 23 minutes or until toothpick inserted in center comes out clean. Cool in pans 5 minutes. Remove to cooling racks. Cool completely. Frost cupcakes with Vanilla frosting. Decorate with fruit snack shapes, if desired. *Makes 12 to 16 servings*

Variation: To make a Berry Surprise Cake, prepare cake following package directions. Pour half the batter into prepared 13×9×2-inch pan. Place 4 fruit snack sheets evenly on top. Pour remaining batter over all. Bake and cool as directed on package. Frost and decorate as directed above.

Berry Surprise Cupcakes

Cookies 'n' Cream Cake

1 package (18¼ ounces) white cake mix
1 package (4-serving size) instant white chocolate pudding and pie
filling mix
1 cup vegetable oil
4 egg whites
½ cup milk
20 chocolate sandwich cookies, coarsely chopped
½ cup semisweet chocolate chips
1 teaspoon shortening
4 chocolate sandwich cookies, cut into quarters for garnish

1. Preheat oven to 350°F. Lightly grease 10-inch bundt pan.

2. Combine cake mix, pudding mix, oil, egg whites and milk in large bowl. Beat with electric mixer at medium speed 2 minutes or until well blended. Stir in chopped cookies; spread in prepared pan.

3. Bake 50 to 60 minutes or until cake springs back when lightly touched and toothpick inserted near center comes out clean. Cool 1 hour in pan on wire rack. Invert cake onto serving plate; cool completely.

4. Combine chocolate chips and shortening in small microwavable bowl. Microwave at HIGH 1 minute; stir. Microwave at 15 second intervals, stirring after each interval, until melted and smooth. Drizzle glaze over cake; garnish with quartered cookies.

Makes 10 to 12 servings

Cookies 'n' Cream Cake

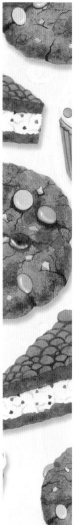

Football Cake

1 package DUNCAN HINES® Moist Deluxe® Devil's Food Cake Mix

Decorator Frosting
¾ cup confectioners' sugar
2 tablespoons shortening plus additional for greasing
1 tablespoon non-dairy powdered creamer
1 tablespoon cold water
¼ teaspoon vanilla extract
   Dash salt
1 container DUNCAN HINES® Creamy Home-Style Chocolate Frosting

1. Preheat oven to 350°F. Grease and flour 10-inch round cake pan. Prepare cake following package directions for basic recipe. Bake at 350°F for 45 to 55 minutes or until toothpick inserted in center comes out clean. Cool completely.

2. For decorator frosting, combine confectioners' sugar, shortening, non-dairy powdered creamer, water, vanilla extract and salt in small bowl. Beat at medium speed with electric mixer 2 minutes. Add more confectioners' sugar to thicken or water to thin frosting as needed.

3. Cut 2-inch wide piece from center of cake; remove. Place cake halves together to make football shape as shown. Spread chocolate frosting on sides and top of cake. Place basketweave tip in pastry bag. Fill with decorator frosting. Make white frosting laces on football. *Makes 12 to 16 servings*

Note: If a 10-inch round pan is not available, make 2 football cakes by following package directions for baking with two 9-inch round cake pans.

Football Cake

Flapjack Party Stack

1 package (18¼ ounces) yellow cake mix, plus ingredients to prepare mix
1 container (16 ounces) vanilla frosting, divided
1 quart fresh strawberries, washed, hulled and sliced
1 cup caramel or butterscotch ice cream topping

1. Preheat oven to 350°F. Grease bottoms and sides of 4 (9-inch) round cake pans; line bottoms with waxed paper. Prepare and bake cake mix according to package directions. Let cakes cool in pans on wire racks 15 minutes. Remove from pans; cool completely.

2. Reserve ¼ cup frosting. Place 1 cake layer on serving plate; spread or pipe ⅓ of remaining frosting in swirls on cake to resemble whipped butter. Top with sliced strawberries. Repeat with next 2 cake layers, frosting and strawberries. Top stack with remaining cake layer.

3. Warm caramel topping in microwave just until pourable. Drizzle over cake. Spread or pipe remaining frosting in center; garnish with remaining strawberries.

Makes 12 servings

Quick Rocky Road Cake

1 package DUNCAN HINES® Moist Deluxe® Devil's Food Cake Mix
1 container DUNCAN HINES® Creamy Home-Style Classic Vanilla Frosting
½ cup creamy peanut butter
⅓ cup semi-sweet chocolate chips
⅓ cup salted cocktail peanuts

1. Preheat oven to 350°F. Grease and flour 13×9×2-inch pan.

2. Prepare, bake and cool cake following package directions for basic recipe.

3. Combine Vanilla Frosting and peanut butter in medium bowl. Frost top of cake. Sprinkle with chocolate chips and peanuts.

Makes 12 to 16 servings

Flapjack Party Stack

Cinnamon Stars

2 tablespoons sugar
¾ teaspoon ground cinnamon
¾ cup butter or margarine, softened
2 egg yolks
1 teaspoon vanilla extract
1 package DUNCAN HINES® Moist Deluxe® French Vanilla Cake Mix

1. Preheat oven to 375°F. Combine sugar and cinnamon in small bowl. Set aside.

2. Combine butter, egg yolks and vanilla extract in large bowl. Blend in cake mix gradually. Roll dough to ⅛-inch thickness on lightly floured surface. Cut with 2½-inch star cookie cutter. Place cutouts 2 inches apart on ungreased baking sheet.

3. Sprinkle cookies with cinnamon-sugar mixture. Bake at 375°F for 6 to 8 minutes or until edges are light golden brown. Cool 1 minute on baking sheet. Remove to cooling rack. Cool completely. Store in airtight container.

Makes 3 to 3½ dozen cookies

Hint: You can use your favorite cookie cutter in place of the star cookie cutter.

Light Up the Sky Cake

1 package (18.25 ounces) any flavor cake mix, plus ingredients to prepare mix
¼ cup (½ stick) butter, softened
2½ cups powdered sugar, divided
2 to 3 tablespoons milk
¼ teaspoon vanilla extract
Blue food coloring
1½ cups "M&M's"® Chocolate Mini Baking Bits

Prepare and bake cake as directed on package for 13×9-inch cake. Cool cake completely on wire rack. In large bowl beat butter until light and fluffy. Add 1¼ cups powdered sugar; beat until fluffy. Blend in milk and vanilla. Beat in remaining 1¼ cups powdered sugar until frosting is smooth. Add enough food coloring to make frosting dark blue. Frost cake and decorate with "M&M's"® Chocolate Mini Baking Bits to look like exploding fireworks. *Makes 16 to 20 servings*

Cinnamon Stars

Surprise Package Cupcakes

1 package (18¼ ounces) chocolate cake mix, plus ingredients to prepare mix
Food coloring (optional)
1 container (16 ounces) vanilla frosting
1 tube (4¼ ounces) white decorator icing
72 chewy fruit squares
Colored decors and birthday candles (optional)

1. Line standard (2½-inch) muffin cups with paper liners or spray with nonstick cooking spray. Prepare and bake cake mix in prepared muffin cups according to package directions. Cool in pans on wire racks 15 minutes. Remove from pans; cool completely on wire racks.

2. If desired, tint frosting with food coloring, adding a few drops at a time until desired color is reached. Frost cupcakes with white or tinted frosting.

3. Use decorator icing to pipe "ribbons" on fruit squares to resemble wrapped presents. Place 3 candy presents on each cupcake. Decorate with decors and candles, if desired. *Makes 24 cupcakes*

Double Chocolate Snack Cake

1 package DUNCAN HINES® Moist Deluxe® Devil's Food Cake Mix
1 cup white chocolate chips, divided
½ cup semisweet chocolate chips

1. Preheat oven to 350°F. Grease and flour 13×9-inch pan.

2. Prepare cake mix as directed on package. Stir in ½ cup white chocolate chips and semisweet chocolate chips. Pour into prepared pan. Bake at 350°F for 35 to 40 minutes or until toothpick inserted in center comes out clean. Remove from oven; sprinkle top with remaining ½ cup white chocolate chips. Serve warm or cool completely in pan. *Makes 12 to 16 servings*

Hint: For a special dessert, serve cake warm with a scoop of vanilla ice cream or whipped cream garnished with chocolate chips.

Surprise Package Cupcakes

Ballet Slippers

**1 package (18¼ ounces) white pudding-in-the-mix cake mix, plus
   ingredients to prepare mix
1 container (16 ounces) vanilla frosting
   Red food coloring
1 tube (4¼ ounces) pink decorator icing
   Pink ribbon**

1. Prepare cake mix and bake in 13×9-inch baking pan according to package directions. Cool completely. Remove from pan. Place on baking sheet; freeze overnight.

2. Cut frozen cake in half lengthwise, then cut each half into ballet slipper shape as shown in photo. Arrange slippers on serving platter. Remaining cake pieces can be frozen for another use.

3. Reserve ⅓ cup frosting. Tint remaining frosting with red food coloring to desired shade of pink. Frost center of each shoe with reserved white frosting, leaving 1 inch on each side and 3 inches at toe. Frost rest of slippers with pink frosting as shown in photo. To add texture, lightly press cheesecloth into frosting and lift off. Outline soles and centers of shoes with pink decorator icing.

4. Tie ribbon into two bows; place on toes of ballet shoes before serving.

Makes 12 to 16 servings

Ballet Slippers

Fudgy Banana Oat Cake

Topping
    1 cup QUAKER® Oats (quick or old fashioned, uncooked)
    ½ cup firmly packed brown sugar
    ¼ cup (½ stick) margarine or butter, chilled

Filling
    1 cup (6 ounces) semisweet chocolate pieces
    ⅔ cup sweetened condensed milk (not evaporated milk)
    1 tablespoon margarine or butter

Cake
    1 package (18.25 ounces) devil's food cake mix
1 ¼ cups mashed ripe bananas (about 3 large)
    ⅓ cup vegetable oil
    3 eggs
    Banana slices (optional)
    Sweetened whipped cream (optional)

Heat oven to 350°F. Lightly grease bottom only of 13×9-inch baking pan. For topping, combine oats and brown sugar. Cut in margarine until mixture is crumbly; set aside.

For filling, in small saucepan, heat chocolate pieces, sweetened condensed milk and margarine over low heat until chocolate is melted, stirring occasionally. Remove from heat; set aside.

For cake, in large mixing bowl, combine cake mix, bananas, oil and eggs. Blend at low speed of electric mixer until dry ingredients are moistened. Beat at medium speed 2 minutes. Spread batter evenly into prepared pan. Drop chocolate filling by teaspoonfuls evenly over batter. Sprinkle with reserved oat topping. Bake 40 to 45 minutes or until cake pulls away from sides of pan and topping is golden brown. Cool cake in pan on wire rack. Cut into squares. Garnish with banana slices and sweetened whipped cream, if desired. *Makes 15 servings*

Fudgy Banana Oat Cake

Ice Cream Cone Cupcakes

1 package (18¼ ounces) white cake mix, plus ingredients to prepare mix
2 tablespoons nonpareils*
24 flat-bottomed ice cream cones
Prepared vanilla and chocolate frostings
Additional nonpareils and decors

Nonpareils are tiny, round, brightly colored sprinkles used for cake and cookie decorating.

1. Preheat oven to 350°F.

2. Prepare cake mix according to package directions. Stir in nonpareils.

3. Spoon ¼ cup batter into each ice cream cone.

4. Stand cones on cookie sheet. Bake cones about 20 minutes or until toothpicks inserted into centers come out clean. Cool on wire racks.

5. Frost cupcakes and decorate as desired. *Makes 24 cupcakes*

Note: Cupcakes are best served the day they are prepared. Store loosely covered.

Porcupine Cupcakes

1 package DUNCAN HINES® Moist Deluxe® Cake Mix (any flavor)
1 container DUNCAN HINES® Chocolate Frosting
Sliced almonds

1. Preheat oven to 350°F. Place 2½-inch paper liners in 24 muffin cups.

2. Prepare, bake and cool cupcakes following package directions for basic recipe. Frost cupcakes with Chocolate frosting. Place sliced almonds upright on each cupcake to decorate as a "porcupine." *Makes 24 cupcakes*

Note: Slivered almonds can be used in place of sliced almonds.

Ice Cream Cone Cupcakes

Back-To-School Pencil Cake

1 package DUNCAN HINES® Moist Deluxe® Cake Mix (any flavor)
2 containers DUNCAN HINES® Creamy Home-Style Classic Vanilla
   Frosting, divided
Red and yellow food coloring
Chocolate sprinkles

1. Preheat oven to 350°F. Grease and flour 13×9×2-inch pan.

2. Prepare, bake and cool cake following package directions for basic recipe.

3. For frosting, tint 1 cup Vanilla frosting pink with red food coloring. Tint remaining frosting with yellow food coloring.

4. To assemble, cut cooled cake and arrange on large baking sheet or piece of sturdy cardboard as shown. Spread pink frosting on cake for eraser at one end and for wood at other end. Spread yellow frosting over remaining cake. Decorate with chocolate sprinkles for pencil tip and eraser band (see photo).

Makes 12 to 16 servings

Hint: To make this cake even more special, reserve ¼ cup Vanilla frosting before tinting yellow. Place writing tip in decorating bag. Fill with frosting. Pipe name of child, teacher or school on pencil.

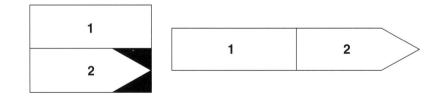

Back-To-School Pencil Cake

Sunflower Cake

1 package (18¼ ounces) chocolate cake mix, plus ingredients to prepare mix
1⅓ cups mini semisweet chocolate chips, divided
1 container (16 ounces) vanilla frosting
Yellow food coloring
Green candy fruit slices for garnish (optional)

1. Grease and flour 10-cup ovenproof glass bowl. (Bowl should be about 9 inches across top.) Prepare cake mix according to package directions. Bake in prepared bowl 60 to 70 minutes. Cool in bowl on wire rack 30 minutes. Remove from bowl; cool completely on wire rack.

2. Place cake flat side down on serving platter. Place ⅓ cup mini chocolate chips in small microwavable bowl. Microwave at HIGH one minute; stir. Microwave at additional 30-second intervals until chips are completely melted, stirring after each interval. Spread melted chocolate chips on flat top of cake. Place remaining mini chocolate chips upright in melted chocolate to form center of sunflower.

3. Tint frosting desired shade of yellow with food coloring. Starting at bottom, using decorating bag fitted with leaf tip, pipe frosting on remainder of cake to form petals. (Or spread frosting with metal spatula and use back of spoon to "lift" frosting into peaks.) Surround cake with fruit slices, if desired.   *Makes 12 servings*

Sunflower Cake

Chocolate Peanut Butter Cookies

1 package DUNCAN HINES® Moist Deluxe® Devil's Food Cake Mix
¾ cup crunchy peanut butter
2 eggs
2 tablespoons milk
1 cup candy-coated peanut butter pieces

1. Preheat oven to 350°F. Grease baking sheets.

2. Combine cake mix, peanut butter, eggs and milk in large mixing bowl. Beat at low speed with electric mixer until blended. Stir in peanut butter pieces.

3. Drop dough by slightly rounded tablespoonfuls onto prepared baking sheets. Bake 7 to 9 minutes or until lightly browned. Cool 2 minutes on baking sheets. Remove to cooling racks. *Makes about 3½ dozen cookies*

Turtle Cake

1 package DUNCAN HINES® Moist Deluxe® Fudge Marble Cake Mix
6 fun-size chocolate-covered nougat, caramel, peanut candy bars
1 container (16 ounces) DUNCAN HINES® Creamy Home-Style Cream Cheese Frosting, divided
Green food coloring
2 tablespoons slivered almonds
Candy-coated chocolate pieces and white chocolate chips

1. Preheat oven to 350°F. Grease and flour 2½-quart ovenproof glass bowl with rounded bottom.

2. Prepare cake following package directions for original recipe. Pour into prepared bowl. Bake at 350°F for 55 to 60 minutes or until toothpick inserted in center comes out clean. Cool in bowl 20 minutes. Invert onto cooling rack. Cool completely.

3. Place cake on serving plate. Remove 1-inch cake square from upper side of cake for head. Insert 2 fun-size candy bars, flat sides together, into square hole for head. Position remaining 4 candy bars under cake for feet. Reserve 1 teaspoon Cream Cheese frosting. Tint remaining Cream Cheese frosting with green food coloring; frost cake. Sprinkle almonds on top. Place candy-coated chocolate pieces around bottom edge of shell. Attach white chocolate chips to head with reserved frosting for eyes.
Makes 12 to 16 servings

Chocolate Peanut Butter Cookies

Ice Cream Cookie Sandwich

2 pints chocolate chip ice cream, softened
1 package DUNCAN HINES® Moist Deluxe® Dark Chocolate Fudge
Cake Mix
½ cup butter or margarine, softened

1. Line bottom of one 9-inch round cake pan with aluminum foil. Spread ice cream in pan; return to freezer until firm. Run knife around edge of pan to loosen ice cream. Remove from pan; wrap in foil and return to freezer.

2. Preheat oven to 350°F. Line bottom of two 9-inch round cake pans with aluminum foil. Place cake mix in large bowl. Add butter; mix thoroughly until crumbs form. Place half the cake mix in each prepared pan; press lightly. Bake at 350°F for 15 minutes or until browned around edges; do not overbake. Cool 10 minutes; remove from pans. Remove foil from cookie layers; cool completely.

3. To assemble, place one cookie layer on serving plate. Top with ice cream. Peel off foil. Place second cookie layer on top. Wrap in foil and freeze 2 hours. To keep longer, store in airtight container. Let stand at room temperature for 5 to 10 minutes before cutting. *Makes 10 to 12 servings*

Cherry Pudding Cake

1 (18¼-ounce) package yellow cake mix, plus ingredients to
prepare mix
1 (8-ounce) package cream cheese, softened
2 cups milk, divided
1 (3-ounce) package instant vanilla pudding
1 (21-ounce) can cherry pie filling

Prepare cake mix according to package directions. Pour batter into greased 13×9×2-inch baking pan. Bake as directed on package. Let cake cool in pan.

Combine cream cheese and ½ cup milk in small bowl. Beat with electric mixer on medium speed 3 to 4 minutes or until smooth. Add pudding mix and remaining 1½ cups milk; mix well. Let mixture stand until thick. Pour cream cheese mixture over cool cake. Top with cherry pie filling. Refrigerate, covered, until ready to serve. *Makes about 15 servings*

Favorite recipe from **Cherry Marketing Institute**

Ice Cream Cookie Sandwich

Cubcakes

1 package (18¼ ounces) chocolate cake mix, plus ingredients to prepare mix
1 container (16 ounces) chocolate frosting
1 package (5 ounces) chocolate nonpareil candies
72 red cinnamon candies
Chocolate sprinkles
Black decorating gel

1. Place paper or foil baking liners in 24 standard (2½-inch) muffin pan cups or spray muffin pan cups with nonstick cooking spray. Prepare cake mix and bake in prepared muffin pans according to package directions. Cool in pans on wire racks 15 minutes. Remove cupcakes from pans; cool completely on wire racks.

2. Spread chocolate frosting on cooled cupcakes. Place nonpareils at tops of cupcakes to make ears and in center of cupcakes to make muzzles. Place red candies on cupcakes for eyes. Attach red candies to muzzles with frosting for noses. Sprinkle with chocolate sprinkles for fur. Place dots of decorating gel on eyes and pipe gel to make mouths. *Makes 24 cupcakes*

tip

To easily fill muffin cups, place the batter in a 4-cup glass measuring cup. Fill each muffin cup ¾ full. Use a plastic spatula to control the flow of the batter into the muffin cups.

Cubcakes

Ice Cream Cone Cakes

1 package DUNCAN HINES® Moist Deluxe® Cake Mix (any flavor)
1 container DUNCAN HINES® Creamy Home-Style Chocolate Frosting
1 container DUNCAN HINES® Creamy Home-Style Vanilla Frosting
Chocolate sprinkles
Assorted decors
Jelly beans
2 maraschino cherries, for garnish

1. Preheat oven to 350°F. Grease and flour one 8-inch round cake pan and one 8-inch square pan.

2. Prepare cake following package directions for basic recipe. Pour about 2 cups batter into round pan. Pour about 3 cups batter into square pan. Bake at 350°F for 30 to 35 minutes or until toothpick inserted in center comes out clean. Cool following package directions.

3. To assemble, cut cooled round cake in half. Cut cooled square cake in half diagonally. Place round cake halves along 8-inch sides of triangular cakes. Frost "cone" with Chocolate frosting, reserving ½ cup. Place writing tip in pastry bag. Fill with remaining ½ cup Chocolate frosting. Pipe waffle pattern onto "cones." Decorate with chocolate sprinkles. Spread Vanilla frosting on "ice cream." Decorate with assorted decors and jelly beans. Top each with maraschino cherry.

Makes 12 to 16 servings

Hint: Use tip of knife to draw lines in frosting for waffle pattern as guide for piping chocolate frosting.

Ice Cream Cone Cakes

Banana Split Cake

1 package DUNCAN HINES® Moist Deluxe® Banana Supreme Cake Mix
3 eggs
1⅓ cups water
½ cup all-purpose flour
⅓ cup vegetable oil
1 cup mini semisweet chocolate chips
2 to 3 bananas
1 can (16 ounces) chocolate syrup
1 container (8 ounces) frozen whipped topping, thawed
½ cup chopped walnuts
Colored sprinkles
Maraschino cherries with stems, for garnish

1. Preheat oven to 350°F. Grease and flour 13×9×2-inch pan.

2. Combine cake mix, eggs, water, flour and oil in large bowl. Beat at low speed with electric mixer until moistened. Beat at medium speed 2 minutes. Stir in chocolate chips. Pour into prepared pan. Bake at 350°F for 32 to 35 minutes or until toothpick inserted in center comes out clean. Cool completely.

3. Slice bananas. Cut cake into squares; top with banana slices. Drizzle with chocolate syrup. Top with whipped topping, walnuts and sprinkles. Garnish with maraschino cherries. *Makes 12 to 16 servings*

Note: Dip bananas in diluted lemon juice to prevent darkening.

Banana Split Cake

Chocolate Confection Cake

1 package DUNCAN HINES® Moist Deluxe® Devil's Food Cake Mix

Filling
- **1 cup evaporated milk**
- **1 cup granulated sugar**
- **24 large marshmallows**
- **1 package (14 ounces) flaked coconut**

Topping
- **½ cup butter or margarine**
- **¼ cup plus 2 tablespoons milk**
- **⅓ cup unsweetened cocoa powder**
- **1 pound confectioners' sugar (3½ to 4 cups)**
- **1 teaspoon vanilla extract**
- **¾ cup sliced almonds**

1. Preheat oven to 350°F. Grease and flour 15½×10½×1-inch jelly-roll pan.

2. Prepare cake following package directions for basic recipe. Pour into prepared pan. Bake at 350°F for 20 to 25 minutes or until toothpick inserted in center comes out clean.

3. For filling, combine evaporated milk and granulated sugar in large saucepan. Bring mixture to a boil. Add marshmallows and stir until melted. Stir in coconut. Spread on warm cake.

4. For topping, combine butter, milk and cocoa in medium saucepan. Stir on low heat until butter is melted. Add confectioners' sugar and vanilla extract, stirring until smooth. Stir in almonds (see Hint). Pour over filling. Spread evenly to edges. Cool completely. *Makes 20 to 24 servings*

Hint: For a pretty presentation, sprinkle the ¾ cup almond slices over topping instead of stirring almonds into topping.

Chocolate Confection Cake

Captivating Caterpillar Cupcakes

1 package DUNCAN HINES® Moist Deluxe® White Cake Mix
3 egg whites
1 ⅓ cups water
2 tablespoons vegetable oil
½ cup star decors, divided
1 container DUNCAN HINES® Vanilla Frosting
Green food coloring
6 chocolate sandwich cookies, finely crushed (see Hint)
½ cup candy-coated chocolate pieces
⅓ cup assorted jelly beans
Assorted nonpareil decors

1. Preheat oven to 350°F. Place paper liners in 24 (2½-inch) muffin cups.

2. Combine cake mix, egg whites, water and oil in large bowl. Beat at low speed with electric mixer until moistened. Beat at medium speed 2 minutes. Fold in ⅓ cup star decors. Fill paper liners about half full. Bake at 350°F for 18 to 23 minutes or until toothpick inserted in center comes out clean. Cool in pans 5 minutes. Remove to cooling racks. Cool completely.

3. Tint Vanilla frosting with green food coloring. Frost one cupcake. Sprinkle ½ teaspoon chocolate cookie crumbs on frosting. Arrange 4 candy-coated chocolate pieces to form caterpillar body. Place jelly bean at one end to form head. Attach remaining star and nonpareil decors with dots of frosting to form eyes. Repeat with remaining cupcakes.   *Makes 24 cupcakes*

Hint: To finely crush chocolate sandwich cookies, place cookies in resealable plastic bag. Remove excess air from bag; seal. Press rolling pin on top of cookies to break into pieces. Continue pressing until evenly crushed

Captivating Caterpillar Cupcakes

Fun Fort

1 package (18¼ ounces) devil's food cake mix, plus ingredients to prepare mix
1 container (16 ounces) chocolate fudge frosting
6 square chocolate-covered snack cakes
9 cream-filled pirouette cookies
1 tube (4¼ ounces) chocolate decorator icing with tips
1 tube (4¼ ounces) white decorator icing with tips
1 tube (4¼ ounces) green decorator icing with tips
Sprinkles
Paper flag and plastic figurines (optional)

1. Prepare and bake cake mix in two 8-inch square baking pans according to package directions. Cool in pans on wire racks 15 minutes. Remove from pans; cool completely.

2. Place 1 cake layer upside down on serving platter; frost top. Place second layer upside down on first cake layer so cake top is completely flat. Frost top and sides. Place one square snack cake in each corner of large cake. Cut remaining two snack cakes in half diagonally; place 1 half cut side down on each snack cake in corners.

3. Attach pirouette cookies with chocolate icing to four corners of cake for fence posts, front gate and flagpole. Decorate fort with chocolate, white and green icings and sprinkles as desired. Attach flag to flagpole with chocolate icing and place figurines on top of cake, if desired. *Makes 12 servings*

Note: Remove inedible objects before serving.

Fun Fort

Rainbow Cake

1 package (18¼ ounces) cake mix (any flavor), plus ingredients to prepare mix
⅓ cup raspberry jam
1 container (16 ounces) vanilla frosting
Multi-colored fruit candies (at least 5 different colors)

1. Prepare and bake cake mix in 2 (8-inch) round cake pans according to package directions. Cool in pans on wire racks 15 minutes. Remove from pans; cool completely on wire racks.

2. Place 1 cake layer upside down on serving platter. Spread raspberry jam over top. Add second cake layer upside down to make flat cake top. Frost entire cake with vanilla frosting.

3. Place string in straight line across center of cake; lift string to remove. Using line left by string as guide, position row of red candies across cake and down side. Place row of orange candies on both sides of red row across top and down side. Repeat with remaining candies in order of colors of the rainbow: yellow, green, violet. Add row of candies around base of cake, alternating colors.   *Makes 12 servings*

Variation: This exceptionally easy cake leaves lots of room for personal creativity. Instead of a rainbow, position the candies in spokes like a color wheel or in diagonal stripes spaced an inch or two apart. Or simply sprinkle the top of the cake with candies for a festive polka dot look.

Rainbow Cake

Princess Castle

**2 packages (18¼ ounces each) cake mix, any flavor, plus
    ingredients to prepare mix**
5 cups Buttercream Frosting (page 110)
3 sugar ice cream cones
   Blue and red or pink food colorings
4 sugar wafer cookies
2 stick pretzels
4 vanilla wafer cookies, cut in half
   Assorted candies, striped fruit gum and assorted decors

1. Prepare and bake cake mix in 4 (9-inch) square baking pans according to package directions. Cool in pans on wire racks 15 minutes. Remove from pans; cool completely on wire racks. Prepare 2 recipes Buttercream Frosting.

2. Cut 4-inch square out of center of three cake layers. Using cut-out squares and remaining cake layer, cut 3-inch triangle for door arch. Use 2-inch cookie or biscuit cutter to cut out 10 circles for towers.

3. Fill and frost first three layers; place on serving plate. If desired, cut out doorway, as shown in photo, on one side of cake; frost opening. Attach cake triangle over door with frosting to form arch. Stack cake circles at corners of castle to form towers. Frost arch and towers. Attach sugar cones on top of frosted towers as shown in photo.

4. Tint ½ cup frosting blue. Pipe bricks, windows and castle trim. Tint ¼ cup frosting pink. Pipe accents on door arch and at base of cone towers. Make drawbridge with sugar wafers and pretzels. Place vanilla wafer halves around base of castle. Use assorted candies, striped gum and decors to decorate castle as desired.

Makes 24 servings

continued on page 110

Princess Castle

Princess Castle, continued

Buttercream Frosting

6 cups powdered sugar, sifted
¾ cup (1½ sticks) butter, softened
¼ cup shortening
6 to 8 tablespoons milk
1 teaspoon vanilla

Combine 3 cups powdered sugar, butter, shortening, 4 tablespoons milk and vanilla in large bowl. Beat with electric mixer until smooth. Add remaining powdered sugar; beat until light and fluffy, adding more milk 1 tablespoon at a time, as needed for good spreading consistency. *Makes about 3 cups frosting*

Snowy Owl Cupcakes

1 package (18¼ ounces) white cake mix, plus ingredients to
prepare mix
1 container (16 ounces) vanilla frosting
2½ cups sweetened shredded coconut
48 round gummy candies
24 chocolate-covered coffee beans or black jelly beans
Black decorating gel

1. Line standard (2½-inch) muffin pan cups with paper liners or spray with nonstick cooking spray. Prepare and bake cake mix in prepared muffin cups according to package directions. Cool in pans on wire racks 15 minutes. Remove from pans; cool completely.

2. Frost cupcakes with vanilla frosting. Sprinkle coconut over each cupcake, covering completely. Place 2 gummy candies on each cupcake for eyes. Add chocolate-covered coffee bean for beak. Use piping gel for pupils. *Makes 24 cupcakes*

Snowy Owl Cupcakes

cupcakes & such

Cappuccino Cupcakes

1 package (about 18 ounces) dark chocolate cake mix
1⅓ cups strong brewed or instant coffee, at room temperature
3 eggs
⅓ cup vegetable oil or melted butter
1 container (16 ounces) vanilla frosting
2 tablespoons coffee liqueur
   Additional coffee liqueur (optional)
   Grated chocolate*
   Chocolate-covered coffee beans (optional)

Grate half of a 3- or 4-ounce milk, dark or espresso chocolate candy bar on the large holes of a grater.

1. Preheat oven to 350°F. Line 24 standard (2½-inch) muffin pan cups with foil or paper baking cups.

2. Beat cake mix, coffee, eggs and oil with electric mixer at low speed 30 seconds. Beat at medium speed 2 minutes.

3. Spoon batter into prepared muffin cups filling ⅔ full. Bake 18 to 20 minutes or until toothpicks inserted into centers come out clean. Cool in pans on wire racks 10 minutes. Remove cupcakes to racks; cool completely. (At this point, cupcakes may be frozen up to 3 months. Thaw at room temperature before frosting.)

4. Combine frosting and 2 tablespoons liqueur in small bowl; mix well. Before frosting, poke about 10 holes in each cupcake with toothpick. Pour 1 to 2 teaspoons liqueur over top of each cupcake, if desired. Frost and sprinkle with grated chocolate. Garnish with chocolate-covered coffee beans, if desired. *Makes 24 cupcakes*

Cappuccino Cupcakes

Pretty-in-Pink Peppermint Cupcakes

1 package (about 18 ounces) white cake mix
1⅓ cups water
3 egg whites
2 tablespoons vegetable oil or melted butter
½ teaspoon peppermint extract
3 to 4 drops red liquid food coloring *or* ¼ teaspoon gel food coloring
1 container (16 ounces) prepared vanilla frosting
½ cup crushed peppermint candies (about 16 candies)

1. Preheat oven to 350°F. Line 30 standard (2½-inch) muffin pan cups with pink or white paper baking cups.

2. Beat cake mix, water, egg whites, oil, peppermint extract and food coloring with electric mixer at low speed 30 seconds. Beat at medium speed 2 minutes.

3. Spoon batter into prepared muffin cups filling ¾ full. Bake 20 to 22 minutes or until toothpicks inserted into centers come out clean. Cool in pans on wire racks 10 minutes. Remove cupcakes to racks; cool completely. (At this point, cupcakes may be frozen up to 3 months. Thaw at room temperature before frosting.)

4. Spread cooled cupcakes with frosting; sprinkle with crushed candies. Store at room temperature up to 24 hours or cover and refrigerate up to 3 days before serving. *Makes about 30 cupcakes*

Pretty-in-Pink Peppermint Cupcakes

Donut Spice Cakes

1 package (9 ounces) yellow cake mix
½ cup cold water
2 eggs
½ teaspoon ground cinnamon
¼ teaspoon ground nutmeg
2 teaspoons powdered sugar

1. Preheat oven to 350°F. Lightly grease and flour 10 (½-cup) mini bundt pans.

2. Combine cake mix, water, eggs, cinnamon and nutmeg in medium bowl. Beat with electric mixer at high speed 4 minutes or until well blended.

3. Spoon about ¼ cup batter into each of 10 prepared bundt pan sections. Bake 13 minutes or until toothpicks inserted into centers come out clean and cakes spring back when touched lightly.

4. Cool in pans on wire racks 5 minutes. Remove cakes from pans. Serve warm or at room temperature. Sprinkle with powdered sugar just before serving.

Makes 10 servings

Prep Time: 10 minutes
Bake Time: 13 minutes

tip

Mini bundt pans are available in many sizes (½-cup, ¾-cup, 1-cup, etc.) and shapes (straight, fluted, flowers, etc.). To make sure that the pan you are using is the size called for in the recipe, measure the amount of water that 1 bundt form will hold.

Donut Spice Cakes

Banana Split Cupcakes

1 package (about 18 ounces) yellow cake mix, divided
1 cup water
1 cup mashed ripe bananas
3 eggs
1 cup chopped drained maraschino cherries
1½ cups miniature semisweet chocolate chips, divided
1½ cups prepared vanilla frosting
1 cup marshmallow creme
1 teaspoon shortening
30 whole maraschino cherries, drained and patted dry

1. Preheat oven to 350°F. Line 30 regular-size (2½-inch) muffin cups with paper baking cups.

2. Reserve 2 tablespoons cake mix. Combine remaining cake mix, water, bananas and eggs in large bowl. Beat at low speed of electric mixer about 30 seconds or until moistened. Beat at medium speed 2 minutes. Combine chopped cherries and reserved cake mix in small bowl. Stir chopped cherry mixture and 1 cup chocolate chips into batter.

3. Spoon batter into prepared muffin cups. Bake 15 to 20 minutes or until toothpicks inserted into centers come out clean. Cool in pans on wire racks 10 minutes. Remove to wire racks; cool completely.

4. Combine frosting and marshmallow creme in medium bowl until well blended. Frost cupcakes.

5. Combine remaining ½ cup chocolate chips and shortening in small microwavable bowl. Microwave at HIGH 30 to 45 seconds, stirring after 30 seconds, or until smooth. Drizzle chocolate mixture over cupcakes. Place one whole cherry on each cupcake. *Makes 30 cupcakes*

Note: If desired, omit chocolate drizzle and top cupcakes with colored sprinkles.

Banana Split Cupcakes

Boston Babies

1 package (18¼ ounces) yellow cake mix
3 eggs *or* ¾ cup cholesterol-free egg substitute
⅓ cup unsweetened applesauce
1 package (4-serving size) sugar-free vanilla pudding and pie filling mix
2 cups low-fat (1%) milk or fat-free (skim) milk
⅓ cup sugar
⅓ cup unsweetened cocoa powder
1 tablespoon cornstarch
1½ cups water
1½ teaspoons vanilla

1. Line 24 (2½-inch) muffin cups with paper liners; set aside.

2. Prepare cake mix according to lower fat package directions, using 3 eggs and applesauce. Spoon batter into prepared muffin cups. Bake according to package directions; cool completely. Freeze 12 cupcakes for another use.

3. Prepare pudding mix according to package directions, using 2 cups milk; cover and refrigerate.

4. For chocolate glaze, combine sugar, cocoa, cornstarch and water in large microwavable bowl; whisk until smooth. Microwave at HIGH 4 to 6 minutes, stirring every 2 minutes, until slightly thickened. Stir in vanilla.

5. To serve, for each dessert drizzle 2 tablespoons chocolate glaze onto plate. Cut 1 cupcake in half; place halves on top of glaze. Top with about 2 heaping tablespoonfuls pudding. Garnish as desired. Serve immediately.

Makes 12 servings (1 cupcake each)

Boston Baby

Pumpkin Bundtings with Apple Cider Glaze

Cakes

>   1 package (about 18 ounces) spice cake mix
>   1 can (16 ounces) solid pack pumpkin (not pumpkin pie filling)
> 1⅓ cups water
>   3 eggs
>   ⅓ cup vegetable oil
>   1 teaspoon vanilla, butter and nut flavoring

Glaze

>   4 cups plus 2 tablespoons apple cider, divided
> 16 whole cloves
>   4 cinnamon sticks *or* 2 teaspoons ground cinnamon
> 1½ teaspoons cornstarch
>   ¾ cup caramel ice cream topping (optional)

1. Preheat oven to 350°F. Grease and flour 12 (½-cup) mini bundt pans.

2. For cakes, combine all cake ingredients in large bowl; mix well. Spoon batter equally into prepared pans. Bake 30 minutes or until toothpicks inserted into centers come out clean. Cool in pans on wire racks 15 minutes. Remove cakes from pans; cool completely on wire racks.

3. For glaze, combine 4 cups apple cider, cloves and cinnamon sticks in nonstick skillet; bring to a boil over high heat. Boil 7 minutes or until liquid has reduced to 1 cup. Meanwhile, combine remaining 2 tablespoons apple cider and cornstarch in small bowl; stir until cornstarch is dissolved.

4. When cider mixture is reduced, add cornstarch mixture; cook and stir until slightly thickened. Remove from heat; cool completely.

5. Remove cloves and cinnamon sticks from glaze; discard. Spoon about 1 tablespoon apple cider glaze over each cake. Drizzle 1 tablespoon caramel topping around outer edge of each cake, if desired.   *Makes 12 servings*

Pumpkin Bundtings with Apple Cider Glaze

Cherry Cupcakes

1 (18¼-ounce) box chocolate cake mix
3 eggs
1⅓ cups water
½ cup vegetable oil
1 (21-ounce) can cherry pie filling
1 (16-ounce) can vanilla frosting

Prepare cake mix according to package directions, using eggs, water and oil. Spoon batter into 24 paper-lined muffin-pan cups, filling two-thirds full.

Remove 24 cherries from cherry filling; set aside. Spoon generous teaspoon of remaining cherry filling onto center of each cupcake.

Bake in preheated 350°F oven 20 to 25 minutes. Cool in pans on wire racks 10 minutes. Remove from pan. Let cool completely. Frost cupcakes with vanilla frosting. Garnish cupcakes with reserved cherries.   *Makes 24 cupcakes*

Favorite recipe from **Cherry Marketing Institute**

Fudge Rum Balls

1 package DUNCAN HINES® Moist Deluxe® Butter Recipe Fudge Cake Mix
2 cups sifted confectioners' sugar
1 cup finely chopped pecans or walnuts
¼ cup unsweetened cocoa powder
1 tablespoon rum extract
Pecans or walnuts, finely chopped

1. Preheat oven to 375°F. Grease and flour 13×9×2-inch pan. Prepare, bake and cool cake following package directions.

2. Crumble cake into large bowl. Stir with fork until crumbs are fine and uniform in size. Add confectioners' sugar, 1 cup nuts, cocoa and rum extract. Stir until well blended.

3. Shape heaping tablespoonfuls of mixture into balls. Garnish by rolling balls in finely chopped nuts. Press firmly to adhere nuts to balls.   *Makes 6 dozen rum balls*

Note: Substitute rum for rum extract.

Cherry Cupcakes

Lemon Poppy Seed Cupcakes

Cupcakes
   1 package DUNCAN HINES® Moist Deluxe® Lemon Supreme Cake Mix
   3 eggs
1⅓ **cups water**
   ⅓ **cup vegetable oil**
   3 tablespoons poppy seeds

Lemon Frosting
   1 container (16 ounces) DUNCAN HINES® Vanilla Frosting
   1 teaspoon grated lemon peel
   ¼ **teaspoon lemon extract**
   3 to 4 drops yellow food coloring
      Yellow and orange gumdrops for garnish

1. Preheat oven to 350°F. Place paper liners in 30 (2½-inch) muffin cups.

2. For cupcakes, combine cake mix, eggs, water, oil and poppy seeds in large bowl. Beat at medium speed of electric mixer 2 minutes. Fill paper liners about half full. Bake at 350°F for 18 to 21 minutes or until toothpick inserted in center comes out clean. Cool in pans 5 minutes. Remove to cooling racks. Cool completely.

3. For lemon frosting, combine Vanilla frosting, lemon peel and lemon extract in small bowl. Tint with yellow food coloring to desired color. Frost cupcakes with lemon frosting. Decorate with gumdrops. *Makes 30 cupcakes*

tip

Poppy seeds are the very tiny bluish-grey to black ripe seeds of the opium poppy plant, which is native to the Mediterranean region. It takes about 900,000 seeds to make one pound. They are available whole, ground and as a sweetened poppy seed filling.

Lemon Poppy Seed Cupcakes

Angel Almond Cupcakes

1 package DUNCAN HINES® Angel Food Cake Mix
1¼ cups water
2 teaspoons almond extract
1 container DUNCAN HINES® Wild Cherry Vanilla Frosting

1. Preheat oven to 350°F.

2. Combine cake mix, water and almond extract in large bowl. Beat at low speed with electric mixer until moistened. Beat at medium speed for 1 minute. Line medium muffin pans with paper baking cups. Fill muffin cups two-thirds full. Bake at 350°F for 20 to 25 minutes or until golden brown, cracked and dry on top. Remove from muffin pans. Cool completely. Frost with frosting. *Makes 30 to 32 cupcakes*

Golden Apple Cupcakes

1 package (18 to 20 ounces) yellow cake mix
1 cup MOTT'S® Chunky Apple Sauce
⅓ cup vegetable oil
3 eggs
¼ cup firmly packed light brown sugar
¼ cup chopped walnuts
½ teaspoon ground cinnamon
Vanilla Frosting (recipe follows)

Heat oven to 350°F. In bowl, combine cake mix, apple sauce, oil and eggs; blend according to package directions. Spoon batter into 24 paper-lined muffin pan cups. Mix brown sugar, walnuts and cinnamon; sprinkle over prepared batter in muffin cups. Bake 20 to 25 minutes or until toothpick inserted in center comes out clean. Cool in pan 10 minutes. Remove from pan; cool completely on wire rack. Frost cupcakes with Vanilla Frosting. *Makes 24 cupcakes*

Vanilla Frosting: In large bowl, beat 1 package (8 ounces) softened cream cheese until light and creamy; blend in ¼ teaspoon vanilla extract. Beat ½ cup heavy cream until stiff; fold into cream cheese mixture.

Angel Almond Cupcakes

Lazy Daisy Cupcakes

1 package (18 ounces) yellow cake mix, plus ingredients to prepare mix
Yellow food coloring
1 container (16 ounces) vanilla frosting
30 large marshmallows
24 small round candies or gumdrops

1. Line 24 standard (2½-inch) muffin cups with paper liners or spray with nonstick cooking spray. Prepare cake mix and bake in muffin cups according to package directions. Cool in pans on wire racks 15 minutes. Remove from pans; cool completely.

2. Add food coloring to frosting, a few drops at a time, until desired color is reached. Frost cooled cupcakes with tinted frosting.

3. Cut each marshmallow crosswise into 4 pieces. Stretch pieces into petal shapes; place 5 pieces on each cupcake to form flower. Place candy in center of each flower.

Makes 24 cupcakes

Coconut Cupcakes

1 package DUNCAN HINES® Moist Deluxe® Butter Recipe Golden Cake Mix
3 eggs
1 cup (8 ounces) dairy sour cream
⅔ cup cream of coconut
¼ cup butter or margarine, softened
2 containers (16 ounces each) DUNCAN HINES® Coconut Frosting

1. Preheat oven to 375°F. Place paper liners in 36 (2½-inch) muffin cups.

2. Combine cake mix, eggs, sour cream, cream of coconut and butter in large bowl. Beat at low speed with electric mixer until blended. Beat at medium speed 4 minutes. Fill paper liners half full. Bake at 375°F for 17 to 19 minutes or until toothpick inserted into center comes out clean. Cool in pans 5 minutes. Remove to cooling racks. Cool completely.

3. Frost cupcakes.

Makes 36 cupcakes

Lazy Daisy Cupcake

Individual Cheesecake Cups

Crust
> **1 package DUNCAN HINES® Moist Deluxe® Classic Yellow or Devil's Food Cake Mix**
> ¼ **cup margarine or butter, melted**

Cheese Filling
> **2 packages (8 ounces each) cream cheese, softened**
> **3 eggs**
> ¾ **cup sugar**
> **1 teaspoon vanilla extract**

Topping
> **1½ cups dairy sour cream**
> ¼ **cup sugar**
> **1 can (21 ounces) cherry pie filling (optional)**

1. Preheat oven to 350°F. Place foil or paper liners in 24 (2½-inch) muffin cups.

2. For crust, combine cake mix and melted margarine in large bowl. Beat at low speed with electric mixer for 1 minute. Mixture will be crumbly. Divide mixture evenly among muffin cups. Level but do not press.

3. For cheese filling, combine cream cheese, eggs, ¾ cup sugar and vanilla extract in medium bowl. Beat at medium speed with electric mixer until smooth. Spoon evenly into muffin cups. Bake at 350°F for 20 minutes or until set.

4. For topping, combine sour cream and ¼ cup sugar in small bowl. Spoon evenly over cheesecakes. Return to oven for 5 minutes. Cool completely. Garnish each cheesecake with cherry pie filling, if desired. Refrigerate until ready to serve.

Makes 24 servings

Individual Cheesecake Cups

His and Hers Cupcakes

1 package (18¼ ounces) cake mix (any flavor), plus ingredients to prepare mix
1 container (16 ounces) vanilla frosting
3 rolls (¾ ounce each) fruit leather, cut into 4×2⅜-inch strips
12 pieces striped fruit gum
Red food coloring
24 vanilla wafer cookies
Small candies

1. Line 24 standard (2½-inch) muffin cups with paper liners, or spray with nonstick cooking spray. Prepare cake mix and bake in muffin cups according to package directions. Cool in pans on wire racks 15 minutes. Remove cupcakes to wire racks; cool completely.

2. For "His" cupcakes, frost 12 cupcakes. Place 1 strip fruit leather on each frosted cupcake to form shirt collar. Cut gum into tie shapes and place on cupcakes.

3. For "Hers" cupcakes, tint remaining frosting pink with food coloring. Frost remaining cupcakes with tinted frosting. Use dab of frosting to sandwich two vanilla wafers together. Repeat with remaining cookies. Frost cookie sandwiches pink. Top each cupcake with frosted cookie sandwich, placing slightly off-center for crown of hat. Decorate hats with fruit leather and candies. *Makes 24 cupcakes*

His and Hers Cupcakes

Chocolate Tiramisu Cupcakes

Cupcakes
  1 package (18¼ ounces) chocolate cake mix
1¼ cups water
  3 eggs
  ⅓ cup vegetable oil or melted butter
  2 tablespoons instant espresso powder
  2 tablespoons brandy (optional)

Frosting
  8 ounces mascarpone cheese or cream cheese
1½ to 1¾ cups powdered sugar
  2 tablespoons coffee-flavored liqueur
  1 tablespoon unsweetened cocoa powder

1. Preheat oven to 350°F. Line 30 standard (2½-inch) muffin pan cups with paper baking cups.

2. Combine cupcake ingredients in large bowl; beat with electric mixer at low speed 30 seconds. Beat at medium speed 2 minutes.

3. Spoon batter into prepared muffin cups filling ⅔ full. Bake 20 to 22 minutes or until toothpicks inserted into centers come out clean. Cool in pans on wire racks 10 minutes. Remove cupcakes to racks; cool completely. (At this point, cupcakes may be frozen up to 3 months. Thaw at room temperature before frosting.)

4. For frosting, combine mascarpone cheese and 1½ cups powdered sugar in large bowl; beat with electric mixer at medium speed until well blended. Add liqueur; beat until well blended. If frosting is too soft, beat in additional powdered sugar or chill until spreadable.

5. Frost cooled cupcakes with frosting. Place cocoa in strainer; shake over cupcakes. Store at room temperature up to 24 hours or cover and refrigerate for up to 3 days before serving. *Makes 30 cupcakes*

Chocolate Tiramisu Cupcakes

Heavenly Lemon Muffins

1 (16-ounce) package angel food cake mix
3 cups all-purpose flour
4 teaspoons baking powder
½ teaspoon salt
1 cup granulated sugar
⅔ cup skim milk
⅔ cup MOTT'S® Natural Apple Sauce
¼ cup vegetable oil
2 egg whites
2 tablespoons grated lemon peel
2 teaspoons lemon extract
4 drops yellow food coloring (optional)
2 tablespoons powdered sugar (optional)

1. Preheat oven to 375°F. Line 24 (2½-inch) muffin cups with paper liners or spray with nonstick cooking spray.

2. In large bowl, prepare angel food cake mix according to package directions.

3. In another large bowl, combine flour, baking powder and salt.

4. In medium bowl, combine granulated sugar, milk, apple sauce, oil, egg whites, lemon peel, lemon extract and food coloring, if desired.

5. Stir apple sauce mixture into flour mixture just until moistened.

6. Fill each muffin cup ⅓ full with apple sauce batter. Top with angel food cake batter, filling each cup almost full.*

7. Bake 20 minutes or until golden and puffed. Immediately remove from pan; cool completely on wire rack. Sprinkle tops with powdered sugar, if desired.

Makes 24 servings

There will be some angel food cake batter remaining.

Heavenly Strawberry Muffins: Substitute strawberry extract for lemon extract and red food coloring for yellow food coloring, if desired. Omit lemon peel.

**Top to Bottom: Heavenly Lemon Muffins
and Heavenly Strawberry Muffin**

Caramel Apple Cupcakes

1 package (about 18 ounces) butter or yellow cake mix, plus ingredients to prepare mix
1 cup chopped dried apples
   Caramel Frosting (recipe follows)
   Chopped nuts (optional)

1. Preheat oven to 375°F. Line 24 standard (2½-inch) muffin pan cups with paper baking cups.

2. Prepare cake mix according to package directions. Stir in apples. Spoon batter into prepared muffin cups.

3. Bake 15 to 20 minutes or until toothpicks inserted into centers come out clean. Cool in pans on wire racks 10 minutes. Remove to racks; cool completely.

4. Prepare Caramel Frosting. Frost cupcakes. Sprinkle cupcakes with nuts, if desired.

Makes 24 cupcakes

Caramel Frosting

  3 tablespoons butter
  1 cup packed light brown sugar
  ½ cup evaporated milk
  ⅛ teaspoon salt
3¾ cups powdered sugar
  ¾ teaspoon vanilla

1. Melt butter in 2-quart saucepan. Stir in brown sugar, evaporated milk and salt. Bring to a boil, stirring constantly. Remove from heat; cool to lukewarm.

2. Beat in powdered sugar until frosting is of spreading consistency. Beat in vanilla until smooth.

Caramel Apple Cupcakes

Chocolate Peanut Butter Cups

1 package DUNCAN HINES® Moist Deluxe® Swiss Chocolate Cake Mix
**1 container DUNCAN HINES® Creamy Home-Style Classic Vanilla
   Frosting**
½ cup creamy peanut butter
**15 miniature peanut butter cup candies, wrappers removed, cut in
   half vertically**

1. Preheat oven to 350°F. Place paper liners in 30 (2½-inch) muffin cups.

2. Prepare, bake and cool cupcakes following package directions for basic recipe.

3. Combine Vanilla frosting and peanut butter in medium bowl. Stir until smooth. Frost one cupcake. Decorate with peanut butter cup candy, cut side down. Repeat with remaining cupcakes, frosting and candies.   *Makes 30 servings*

Note: You can substitute Duncan Hines® Moist Deluxe® Devil's Food, Dark Chocolate Fudge or Butter Recipe Fudge Cake Mix flavors for Swiss Chocolate Cake Mix.

Golden Oatmeal Muffins

**1 package DUNCAN HINES® Moist Deluxe® Butter Recipe Golden
   Cake Mix**
1 cup uncooked quick-cooking oats (not instant or old-fashioned)
¼ teaspoon salt
¾ cup milk
2 eggs, lightly beaten
2 tablespoons butter or margarine, melted

1. Preheat oven to 400°F. Grease 24 (2½-inch) muffin cups (or use paper liners).

2. Combine cake mix, oats and salt in large bowl. Add milk, eggs and melted butter; stir until moistened. Fill muffin cups two-thirds full. Bake at 400°F for 13 minutes or until golden brown. Cool in pan 5 to 10 minutes. Loosen carefully before removing from pan. Serve with honey or your favorite jam.   *Makes 2 dozen muffins*

Chocolate Peanut Butter Cups

Fudge 'n' Banana Cupcakes

1 package DUNCAN HINES® Moist Deluxe® Devil's Food Cake Mix
3 eggs
1⅓ cups water
½ cup vegetable oil
½ cup (1 stick) butter or margarine
2 ounces (2 squares) unsweetened chocolate
1 pound confectioners' sugar
½ cup half-and-half
1 teaspoon vanilla extract
4 medium bananas
2 tablespoons lemon juice

1. Preheat oven to 350°F. Line 24 muffin cups with paper baking cups. Combine cake mix, eggs, water and oil in large bowl. Prepare, bake and cool cupcakes as directed on package.

2. For frosting,* melt butter and chocolate in heavy saucepan over low heat. Remove from heat. Add confectioners' sugar alternately with half-and-half, mixing until smooth after each addition. Beat in vanilla extract. Add more confectioners' sugar to thicken or half-and-half to thin as needed.

3. Using small paring knife, remove cone-shaped piece from top center of each cupcake. Dot top of each cone with frosting. Frost top of each cupcake spreading frosting down into cone-shaped hole. Slice bananas and dip in lemon juice. Stand three banana slices in each hole. Set cone-shaped pieces, pointed side up, on banana slices. *Makes 24 cupcakes*

*Or use 1 can DUNCAN HINES® Chocolate Frosting.

Cream-Filled Banana Cupcakes

Cream Cheese Filling (recipe follows)
1 package (18.5 ounces) banana cake mix
¾ cup finely chopped nuts
2 tablespoons sugar

1. Prepare Cream Cheese Filling; set aside. Heat oven to 350°F.

2. Prepare cake batter according to package directions. Fill paper-lined muffin cups (2½ inches in diameter) ½ full with batter. Spoon about 1 teaspoonful filling into center of each cupcake. Combine nuts and sugar; sprinkle about 1 teaspoonful over top of each cupcake.

3. Bake 20 minutes or until wooden pick inserted in cake portion comes out clean. Cool on wire rack. *Makes about 3 dozen cupcakes*

Cream Cheese Filling

1 package (8 ounces) cream cheese, softened
⅓ cup sugar
1 egg
1 cup HERSHEY'S MINI CHIPS™ Semi-Sweet Chocolate Chips

1. Combine cream cheese, sugar and egg in small bowl; beat until smooth. Stir in small chocolate chips.

the cookie jar

Choco-Scutterbotch

⅔ **Butter Flavor CRISCO® Stick or ⅔ cup Butter Flavor CRISCO®**
   all-vegetable shortening
½ **cup firmly packed light brown sugar**
 2 **eggs**
 1 **package (18¼ ounces) deluxe yellow cake mix**
 1 **cup toasted rice cereal**
½ **cup butterscotch chips**
½ **cup milk chocolate chunks**
½ **cup semisweet chocolate chips**
½ **cup coarsely chopped walnuts or pecans**

1. Heat oven to 375°F. Place sheets of foil on countertop for cooling cookies.

2. Combine ⅔ cup shortening and brown sugar in large bowl. Beat at medium speed of electric mixer until well blended. Beat in eggs.

3. Add cake mix gradually at low speed. Mix until well blended. Stir in cereal, butterscotch chips, chocolate chunks, chocolate chips and nuts. Stir until well blended.

4. Shape dough into 1¼-inch balls. Place 2 inches apart on ungreased baking sheet. Flatten slightly. Shape sides to form circle, if necessary.

5. Bake for 7 to 9 minutes or until lightly browned around edges. *Do not overbake.* Cool 2 minutes on baking sheet. Remove cookies to foil to cool completely.

Makes 3 dozen cookies

Choco-Scutterbotch

Chocolate Almond Biscotti

1 package DUNCAN HINES® Moist Deluxe® Dark Chocolate Cake Mix
1 cup all-purpose flour
½ cup butter or margarine, melted
2 eggs
1 teaspoon almond extract
½ cup chopped almonds
    White chocolate, melted (optional)

1. Preheat oven to 350°F. Line 2 baking sheets with parchment paper.

2. Combine cake mix, flour, butter, eggs and almond extract in large bowl. Beat at low speed with electric mixer until well blended; stir in almonds. Divide dough in half. Shape each half into 12×2-inch log; place logs on prepared baking sheets. (Bake logs separately.)

3. Bake at 350°F for 30 to 35 minutes or until toothpick inserted in center comes out clean. Remove logs from oven; cool on baking sheets 15 minutes. Using serrated knife, cut logs into ½-inch slices. Arrange slices on baking sheets. Bake biscotti 10 minutes. Remove to cooling racks; cool completely.

4. Dip one end of each biscotti in melted white chocolate, if desired. Allow white chocolate to set at room temperature before storing biscotti in airtight container.

Makes about 2½ dozen cookies

tip

White chocolate is not really chocolate at all because it lacks chocolate liquor, the main component in unsweetened chocolate. White chocolate is cocoa butter with added sugar, milk and flavorings (often vanilla or vanillin). It is more delicate than other chocolates and burns easily. So melt it carefully using a double boiler and stirring constantly.

Chocolate Almond Biscotti

Coconut Clouds

2⅔ cups flaked coconut, divided
1 package DUNCAN HINES® Moist Deluxe® Classic Yellow Cake Mix
1 egg
½ cup vegetable oil
¼ cup water
1 teaspoon almond extract

1. Preheat oven to 350°F. Reserve 1⅓ cups coconut in medium bowl.

2. Combine cake mix, egg, oil, water and almond extract in large bowl. Beat at low speed with electric mixer. Stir in remaining 1⅓ cups coconut. Drop rounded teaspoonful dough into reserved coconut. Roll to cover lightly. Place on ungreased baking sheet. Repeat with remaining dough, placing balls 2 inches apart. Bake at 350°F for 10 to 12 minutes or until light golden brown. Cool 1 minute on baking sheets. Remove to cooling racks. Cool completely. Store in airtight container.

Makes 3½ dozen cookies

Hint: To save time when forming dough into balls, use a 1-inch spring-operated cookie scoop. Spring-operated cookie scoops are available at kitchen specialty shops.

Fudgy Oatmeal Butterscotch Cookies

1 package (18.25 ounces) devil's food cake mix
1½ cups quick-cooking or old-fashioned oats, uncooked
¾ cup (1½ sticks) butter, melted
2 eggs
1 tablespoon vegetable oil
1 teaspoon vanilla extract
1¼ cups "M&M's"® Chocolate Mini Baking Bits
1 cup butterscotch chips

Preheat oven to 350°F. In large bowl combine cake mix, oats, butter, eggs, oil and vanilla until well blended. Stir in "M&M's"® Chocolate Mini Baking Bits and butterscotch chips. Drop by heaping tablespoonfuls about 2 inches apart onto ungreased cookie sheets. Bake 10 to 12 minutes. Cool 1 minute on cookie sheets; cool completely on wire racks. Store in tightly covered container. *Makes about 3 dozen cookies*

Coconut Clouds

Easy Lemon Cookies

1 package DUNCAN HINES® Moist Deluxe® Lemon Cake Mix
2 eggs
½ cup vegetable oil
1 teaspoon grated lemon peel
Pecan halves for garnish

1. Preheat oven to 350°F.

2. Combine cake mix, eggs, oil and lemon peel in large bowl. Stir until well blended. Drop by rounded teaspoonfuls 2 inches apart onto ungreased baking sheets. Press pecan half into center of each cookie. Bake at 350°F for 9 to 11 minutes or until edges are light golden brown. Cool 1 minute on baking sheets. Remove to wire racks. Cool completely. Store in airtight container. *Makes 4 dozen cookies*

Note: You can substitute whole almonds or walnut halves for the pecan halves.

Festive Chocolate Chip Cookies

1 package DUNCAN HINES® Moist Deluxe® Classic White Cake Mix
¼ cup firmly packed light brown sugar
1 egg
¾ cup vegetable oil
1 package (6 ounces) semisweet chocolate chips
½ cup chopped pecans or walnuts
Assorted decors

1. Preheat oven to 350°F.

2. Combine cake mix, brown sugar, egg and oil in large bowl. Beat at low speed with electric mixer until blended. Stir in chocolate chips and pecans. Shape dough into 1½-inch balls. Dip tops of balls in decors. Place 2 inches apart on ungreased baking sheets. Bake at 350°F for 10 to 12 minutes or until light golden brown around edges. Cool 2 minutes on baking sheets. Remove to cooling racks. Cool completely. Store in airtight container. *Makes 3 to 3½ dozen cookies*

Hint: Cool baking sheet completely before baking each batch of cookies.

Easy Lemon Cookies

Crispy Thumbprint Cookies

1 package (18.25 ounces) yellow cake mix
½ cup vegetable oil
¼ cup water
1 egg
3 cups crisp rice cereal, crushed
½ cup chopped walnuts
6 tablespoons raspberry or strawberry preserves

1. Preheat oven to 375°F.

2. Combine cake mix, oil, water and egg. Beat at medium speed of electric mixer until well blended. Add cereal and walnuts; mix until well blended.

3. Drop by heaping teaspoonfuls about 2 inches apart onto ungreased baking sheets. Use thumb to make indentation in each cookie. Spoon about ½ teaspoon preserves into center of each cookie.

4. Bake 9 to 11 minutes or until golden brown. Cool cookies 1 minute on baking sheet; remove from baking sheet to wire rack to cool completely.

Makes 3 dozen cookies

Prep and Cook Time: 30 minutes

Spicy Sour Cream Cookies

1 package DUNCAN HINES® Moist Deluxe® Spice Cake Mix
1 cup sour cream
1 cup chopped pecans or walnuts
¼ cup butter or margarine, softened
1 egg

1. Preheat oven to 350°F. Grease baking sheets.

2. Combine cake mix, sour cream, pecans, butter and egg in large bowl. Beat at low speed with electric mixer until blended.

3. Drop dough by rounded teaspoonfuls onto prepared baking sheets. Bake at 350°F for 9 to 11 minutes or until lightly browned. Cool 2 minutes on baking sheets. Remove to cooling racks; cool completely.   *Makes about 4½ dozen cookies*

Crispy Thumbprint Cookies

Double Nut Chocolate Chip Cookies

1 package DUNCAN HINES® Moist Deluxe® Classic Yellow Cake Mix
½ cup butter or margarine, melted
1 egg
1 cup semisweet chocolate chips
½ cup finely chopped pecans
1 cup sliced almonds, divided

1. Preheat oven to 375°F. Grease baking sheets.

2. Combine cake mix, butter and egg in large bowl. Beat at low speed with electric mixer until just blended. Stir in chocolate chips, pecans and ¼ cup almonds. Shape rounded tablespoonfuls of dough into balls. Place remaining ¾ cup almonds in shallow bowl. Press tops of balls into almonds. Place 1 inch apart on prepared baking sheets.

3. Bake at 375°F for 9 to 11 minutes or until lightly browned. Cool 2 minutes on baking sheets. Remove to cooling racks. *Makes 3 to 3½ dozen cookies*

Triple Chocolate Cookies

1 package DUNCAN HINES® Moist Deluxe® Swiss Chocolate Cake Mix
½ cup butter or margarine, melted
1 egg
½ cup semisweet chocolate chips
½ cup milk chocolate chips
½ cup coarsely chopped white chocolate
½ cup chopped pecans

1. Preheat oven to 375°F.

2. Combine cake mix, butter and egg in large bowl. Beat at low speed with electric mixer until just blended. Stir in all 3 chocolates and pecans.

3. Drop by rounded tablespoonfuls onto ungreased baking sheets. Bake at 375°F for 9 to 11 minutes. Cool 1 minute on baking sheets. Remove to cooling racks.
Makes 3½ to 4 dozen cookies

Note: Cookies can be stored in an airtight container in freezer for up to 6 months.

Double Nut Chocolate Chip Cookies

Spicy Oatmeal Raisin Cookies

1 package DUNCAN HINES® Moist Deluxe® Spice Cake Mix
4 egg whites
1 cup uncooked quick-cooking oats (not instant or old-fashioned)
½ cup vegetable oil
½ cup raisins

1. Preheat oven to 350°F. Grease baking sheets.

2. Combine cake mix, egg whites, oats and oil in large bowl. Beat at low speed with electric mixer until blended. Stir in raisins. Drop by rounded teaspoonfuls onto prepared baking sheets.

3. Bake at 350°F for 7 to 9 minutes or until lightly browned. Cool 1 minute on baking sheets. Remove to cooling racks; cool completely.

Makes about 4 dozen cookies

Vanilla Butter Crescents

1 package DUNCAN HINES® Moist Deluxe® French Vanilla Cake Mix
¾ cup butter, softened
1 vanilla bean, very finely chopped (see Hint)
1 cup finely chopped pecans or walnuts
Confectioners' sugar

1. Preheat oven to 350°F.

2. Place cake mix and butter in large bowl. Cut in butter with pastry blender or 2 knives. Stir in vanilla bean and pecans. (Since mixture is crumbly, it may be helpful to work dough with hands to blend until mixture holds together.) Shape dough into balls. Roll 1 ball between palms until 4 inches long. Shape into crescent. Repeat with remaining dough balls. Place 2 inches apart on ungreased baking sheets. Bake at 350°F for 10 to 12 minutes or until light golden brown around edges. Cool 2 minutes on baking sheets. Remove to cooling racks. Dust with confectioners' sugar. Cool completely. Dust with additional confectioners' sugar, if desired. Store in airtight container.

Makes 4 dozen cookies

Hint: To quickly chop vanilla bean, place in work bowl of food processor fitted with knife blade. Process until fine.

Spicy Oatmeal Raisin Cookies

Quick Fruit & Lemon Drops

1 package (about 18 ounces) lemon cake mix
⅓ cup water
¼ cup butter, softened
1 egg
1 tablespoon grated lemon peel
1 cup mixed dried fruit bits
½ cup sugar

1. Preheat oven to 350°F. Grease cookie sheets.

2. Beat cake mix, water, butter, egg and lemon peel in large bowl with electric mixer at low speed until well blended. Beat in fruit bits just until blended.

3. Place sugar in small bowl. Shape dough by heaping tablespoons into balls; roll in sugar. Place 2 inches apart on prepared cookie sheets.

4. Bake 12 to 14 minutes or until set. Cool on cookie sheets 2 minutes. Transfer to wire racks; cool completely. *Makes about 2 dozen cookies*

Note: If dough is too sticky add about ¼ cup all-purpose flour.

Snickerdoodles

3 tablespoons sugar
1 teaspoon ground cinnamon
1 package DUNCAN HINES® Moist Deluxe® Classic Yellow Cake Mix
2 eggs
¼ cup vegetable oil

1. Preheat oven to 375°F. Grease baking sheets. Place sheets of foil on countertop for cooling cookies.

2. Combine sugar and cinnamon in small bowl.

3. Combine cake mix, eggs and oil in large bowl. Stir until well blended. Shape dough into 1-inch balls. Roll in cinnamon-sugar mixture. Place balls 2 inches apart on baking sheets. Flatten balls with bottom of glass.

4. Bake at 375°F for 8 to 9 minutes or until set. Cool 1 minute on baking sheets. Remove to foil to cool completely. *Makes about 3 dozen cookies*

Quick Fruit & Lemon Drops

Chocolate Oat Chewies

1 package DUNCAN HINES® Moist Deluxe® Devil's Food Cake Mix
1⅓ cups old-fashioned oats, uncooked
1 cup flaked coconut, toasted and divided
¾ cup butter or margarine, melted
2 eggs, beaten
1 teaspoon vanilla extract
5 bars (1.55 ounces each) milk chocolate, cut into rectangles

1. Preheat oven to 350°F.

2. Combine cake mix, oats, ½ cup coconut, butter, eggs and vanilla extract in large bowl. Beat at low speed with electric mixer until blended. Cover and chill 15 minutes.

3. Shape dough into 1-inch balls. Place balls 2 inches apart on ungreased baking sheets. Bake at 350°F for 12 minutes or until tops are slightly cracked. Remove from oven. Press one milk chocolate rectangle into center of each cookie. Sprinkle with remaining ½ cup coconut. Remove to cooling racks. Cool completely.

Makes about 4½ dozen cookies

Butterscotch Spice Cookies

1 package DUNCAN HINES® Moist Deluxe® Spice Cake Mix
2 eggs
½ cup vegetable oil
1 teaspoon vanilla extract
1 cup butterscotch flavored chips

1. Preheat oven to 375°F.

2. Combine cake mix, eggs, oil and vanilla extract in large bowl. Beat at low speed with electric mixer until blended. Stir in butterscotch chips. Drop by rounded teaspoonfuls 2 inches apart onto ungreased baking sheets. Bake at 375°F for 8 to 10 minutes or until set. Cool 2 minutes on baking sheets. Remove to cooling racks. Cool completely. Store in airtight container.

Makes 3 dozen cookies

Note: For chewy cookies, bake for 8 minutes. Cookies will be slightly puffed when removed from the oven and will settle while cooling.

Chocolate Oat Chewies

Chocolate Cherry Cookies

1 package (8 ounces) low-fat sugar-free chocolate cake mix
3 tablespoons fat-free (skim) milk
½ teaspoon almond extract
10 maraschino cherries, rinsed, drained and cut into halves
2 tablespoons white chocolate chips
½ teaspoon canola oil

1. Preheat oven to 350°F. Spray baking sheets with nonstick cooking spray; set aside.

2. Beat cake mix, milk and almond extract in medium bowl with electric mixer at low speed. Increase speed to medium when mixture looks crumbly; beat 2 minutes or until smooth dough forms. (Dough will be very sticky.)

3. Coat hands with cooking spray. Shape dough into 1-inch balls. Place balls 2½ inches apart on prepared baking sheets. Flatten each ball slightly. Place cherry half in center of each cookie.

4. Bake 8 to 9 minutes or until cookies lose their shininess and tops begin to crack. *Do not overbake.* Remove to wire racks; cool completely.

5. Place white chocolate chips and oil in small microwavable bowl. Microwave at HIGH 30 seconds; stir. Repeat as necessary until chips are melted and mixture is smooth. Drizzle white chocolate mixture over cookies. Let stand until set.

Makes 20 servings

Chocolate Cherry Cookies

Chocolate Chip 'n Oatmeal Cookies

1 package (18.25 or 18.5 ounces) yellow cake mix
1 cup quick-cooking rolled oats, uncooked
¾ cup (1½ sticks) butter or margarine, softened
2 eggs
1 cup HERSHEY'S Semi-Sweet Chocolate Chips

1. Heat oven to 350°F.

2. Combine cake mix, oats, butter and eggs in large bowl; mix well. Stir in chocolate chips. Drop by rounded teaspoons onto ungreased cookie sheets.

3. Bake 10 to 12 minutes or until very lightly browned. Cool slightly; remove from cookie sheets to wire racks. Cool completely.   *Makes about 4 dozen cookies*

Cinnamon Crinkles

2 tablespoons sugar
½ teaspoon ground cinnamon
2 eggs, separated
1 teaspoon water
¾ cup butter or margarine, softened
1 teaspoon vanilla extract
1 package DUNCAN HINES® Moist Deluxe® French Vanilla Cake Mix
48 whole almonds or pecan halves for garnish

1. Preheat oven to 375°F. Combine sugar and cinnamon in small bowl; set aside. Combine egg whites and water in another small bowl; beat lightly with fork. Set aside.

2. Combine butter, egg yolks and vanilla extract in large bowl. Blend in cake mix gradually. Beat at low speed with electric mixer until blended. Shape 1 rounded teaspoonful of dough into ball. Dip half the ball into egg white mixture then into cinnamon-sugar mixture. Place ball sugar side up on ungreased baking sheet. Press almond on top. Repeat with remaining dough, placing balls 2 inches apart.

3. Bake at 375°F for 9 to 12 minutes or until edges are light golden brown. Cool 2 minutes on baking sheets. Remove to cooling racks. Store in airtight container.
Makes 4 dozen cookies

Note: Cookies will be slightly puffed when removed from the oven and will settle while cooling.

Chocolate Chip 'n Oatmeal Cookies

Orange Pecan Gems

1 package DUNCAN HINES® Moist Deluxe® Orange Supreme Cake Mix
1 container (8 ounces) vanilla low fat yogurt
1 egg
2 tablespoons butter or margarine, softened
1 cup finely chopped pecans
1 cup pecan halves

1. Preheat oven to 350°F. Grease baking sheets.

2. Combine cake mix, yogurt, egg, butter and chopped pecans in large bowl. Beat at low speed with electric mixer until blended. Drop by rounded teaspoonfuls 2 inches apart onto prepared baking sheets. Press pecan half into center of each cookie. Bake at 350°F for 11 to 13 minutes or until golden brown. Cool 1 minute on baking sheets. Remove to cooling racks. Cool completely. Store in airtight container.

Makes 4½ to 5 dozen cookies

Swiss Chocolate Crispies

1 package DUNCAN HINES® Moist Deluxe® Swiss Chocolate Cake Mix
½ cup shortening plus additional for greasing
½ cup butter or margarine, softened
2 eggs
2 tablespoons water
3 cups crispy rice cereal, divided

1. Combine cake mix, ½ cup shortening, butter, eggs and water in large bowl. Beat at low speed with electric mixer for 2 minutes. Fold in 1 cup cereal. Refrigerate 1 hour.

2. Crush remaining 2 cups cereal into coarse crumbs.

3. Preheat oven to 350°F. Grease baking sheets. Shape dough into 1-inch balls. Roll in crushed cereal. Place on prepared baking sheets about 1 inch apart.

4. Bake at 350°F for 11 to 13 minutes. Cool 1 minute on baking sheets. Remove to wire racks. Cool completely. *Makes about 4 dozen cookies*

Orange Pecan Gems

Quick Chocolate Softies

1 package (about 18 ounces) devil's food cake mix
⅓ cup water
¼ cup butter, softened
1 egg
1 cup white chocolate chips
½ cup coarsely chopped walnuts

Preheat oven to 350°F. Grease cookie sheets. Combine cake mix, water, butter and egg in large bowl. Beat with electric mixer at low speed until moistened. Increase speed to medium; beat 1 minute. (Dough will be stiff.) Stir in white chocolate chips and nuts; stir until well blended. Drop dough by heaping teaspoonfuls 2 inches apart onto prepared cookie sheets.

Bake 10 to 12 minutes or until set. Let cookies stand on cookie sheets 1 minute. Remove cookies to wire racks; cool completely.   *Makes about 4 dozen cookies*

Devil's Food Fudge Cookies

1 package DUNCAN HINES® Moist Deluxe® Devil's Food Cake Mix
2 eggs
½ cup vegetable oil
1 cup semisweet chocolate chips
½ cup chopped walnuts

1. Preheat oven to 350°F. Grease baking sheets.

2. Combine cake mix, eggs and oil in large bowl. Beat until well blended. Stir in chocolate chips and walnuts. (Mixture will be stiff.) Shape dough into 36 (1¼-inch) balls. Place 2 inches apart on prepared baking sheets.

3. Bake at 350°F for 10 to 11 minutes. (Cookies will look moist.) *Do not overbake.* Cool 2 minutes on baking sheets. Remove to cooling racks. Cool completely. Store in airtight container.   *Makes 3 dozen cookies*

Note: For a delicious flavor treat, substitute peanut butter chips for the chocolate chips and chopped peanuts for the chopped walnuts.

Quick Chocolate Softies

Lemon Cookies

1 package DUNCAN HINES® Moist Deluxe® Lemon Supreme Cake Mix
2 eggs
⅓ cup vegetable oil
1 tablespoon lemon juice
¾ cup chopped nuts or flaked coconut
   Confectioners' sugar

1. Preheat oven to 375°F. Grease baking sheets.

2. Combine cake mix, eggs, oil and lemon juice in large bowl. Beat at low speed with electric mixer until well blended. Stir in nuts. Shape dough into 1-inch balls. Place 1 inch apart on prepared baking sheets.

3. Bake at 375°F for 6 to 7 minutes or until lightly browned. Cool 1 minute on baking sheets. Remove to cooling racks. Sprinkle with confectioners' sugar.
Makes about 3 dozen cookies

Note: You can frost cookies with 1 cup confectioners' sugar mixed with 1 tablespoon lemon juice instead of sprinkling cookies with confectioners' sugar.

Quick Peanut Butter Chocolate Chip Cookies

1 package DUNCAN HINES® Moist Deluxe® Classic Yellow Cake Mix
½ cup creamy peanut butter
½ cup butter or margarine, softened
2 eggs
1 cup milk chocolate chips

1. Preheat oven to 350°F. Grease baking sheets.

2. Combine cake mix, peanut butter, butter and eggs in large bowl. Beat at low speed with electric mixer until well blended. Stir in chocolate chips.

3. Drop by rounded teaspoonfuls onto prepared baking sheets. Bake at 350°F for 9 to 11 minutes or until lightly browned. Cool 2 minutes on baking sheets. Remove to cooling racks.
Makes about 4 dozen cookies

Note: Crunchy peanut butter can be substituted for regular peanut butter.

Lemon Cookies

incredible bars

Lemon Cheese Bars

**1 package (18¼ ounces) white or yellow pudding-in-the-mix
    cake mix**
2 eggs
⅓ cup vegetable oil
1 package (8 ounces) cream cheese
⅓ cup sugar
1 teaspoon lemon juice

1. Preheat oven to 350°F.

2. Combine cake mix, 1 egg and oil in large bowl; stir until crumbly. Reserve 1 cup crumb mixture. Press remaining crumb mixture into ungreased 13×9-inch cake pan. Bake 15 minutes or until light golden brown.

3. Combine remaining egg, cream cheese, sugar and lemon juice in medium bowl; beat until smooth and well blended. Spread over baked layer. Sprinkle with reserved crumb mixture. Bake 15 minutes. Cool in pan on wire rack; cut into bars.

Makes 18 bars

tip

When purchasing lemons, look for those that are firm and heavy for their size, with a sheen to the skin. Avoid those that have any sign of green, which indicates that they are not ripe.

Lemon Cheese Bars

Double Chocolate Chewies

1 package DUNCAN HINES® Moist Deluxe® Butter Recipe Fudge Cake Mix
2 eggs
½ cup butter or margarine, melted
1 package (6 ounces) semisweet chocolate chips
1 cup chopped nuts
Confectioners' sugar (optional)

1. Preheat oven to 350°F. Grease 13×9×2-inch baking pan.

2. Combine cake mix, eggs and melted butter in large bowl. Stir until thoroughly blended. (Mixture will be stiff.) Stir in chocolate chips and nuts. Press mixture evenly in prepared pan. Bake at 350°F for 25 to 30 minutes or until toothpick inserted in center comes out clean. *Do not overbake.* Cool completely. Cut into bars. Dust with confectioners' sugar, if desired. *Makes 36 bars*

Banana Gingerbread Bars

1 package (14.5 ounces) gingerbread cake mix
½ cup lukewarm water
1 ripe, medium DOLE® Banana, mashed (about ½ cup)
1 egg
1 small DOLE® Banana, peeled and chopped
½ cup DOLE® Seedless Raisins
½ cup slivered almonds
1½ cups powdered sugar
Juice from 1 lemon

• Preheat oven to 350°F.

• In large bowl, combine gingerbread mix, water, mashed banana and egg. Beat on low speed of electric mixer 1 minute. Stir in chopped banana, raisins and almonds.

• Spread batter in greased 13×9-inch baking pan. Bake 20 to 25 minutes or until top springs back when lightly touched.

• In medium bowl, mix powdered sugar and 3 tablespoons lemon juice to make thin glaze. Spread over warm gingerbread. Cool before cutting into bars. Sprinkle with additional powdered sugar, if desired. *Makes about 32 bars*

Double Chocolate Chewies

Orange Coconut Cream Bars

1 (18¼-ounce) package yellow cake mix
1 cup quick-cooking or old-fashioned oats, uncooked
¾ cup chopped nuts
½ cup butter or margarine, melted
1 egg
1 (14-ounce) can sweetened condensed milk
2 teaspoons grated orange zest
1 cup shredded coconut
1 cup "M&M's"® Semi-Sweet Chocolate Mini Baking Bits

Preheat oven to 375°F. Lightly grease 13×9×2-inch baking pan; set aside. In large bowl combine cake mix, oats, nuts, butter and egg until ingredients are thoroughly moistened and mixture resembles coarse crumbs. Reserve 1 cup mixture. Firmly press remaining mixture onto bottom of prepared pan; bake 10 minutes. In separate bowl combine condensed milk and orange zest; spread over baked base. Combine reserved crumb mixture, coconut and "M&M's"® Semi-Sweet Chocolate Mini Baking Bits; sprinkle evenly over condensed milk mixture and press in lightly. Continue baking 20 to 25 minutes or until golden brown. Cool completely. Cut into bars. Store in tightly covered container. *Makes 26 bars*

Butterscotch Pan Cookies

1 package DUNCAN HINES® Moist Deluxe® French Vanilla Cake Mix
2 eggs
1 cup butter or margarine, melted
¾ cup firmly packed light brown sugar
1 teaspoon vanilla extract
1 package (12 ounces) butterscotch flavored chips
1½ cups chopped pecans

1. Preheat oven to 375°F. Grease 15½×10½×1-inch jelly-roll pan.

2. Combine cake mix, eggs, melted butter, brown sugar and vanilla extract in large bowl. Beat at low speed with electric mixer until smooth and creamy. Stir in butterscotch chips and pecans. Spread in prepared pan. Bake at 375°F for 20 to 25 minutes or until golden brown. Cool completely. Cut into bars. *Makes 48 bars*

Orange Coconut Cream Bars

Pecan Date Bars

Crust
    ⅓ cup shortening plus additional for greasing
    1 package DUNCAN HINES® Moist Deluxe® Classic White Cake Mix
    1 egg

Topping
    1 package (8 ounces) chopped dates
    1¼ cups chopped pecans
    1 cup water
    ½ teaspoon vanilla extract
    Confectioners' sugar

1. Preheat oven to 350°F. Grease and flour 13×9-inch baking pan.

2. For crust, cut ⅓ cup shortening into cake mix with pastry blender or 2 knives until mixture resembles coarse crumbs. Add egg; stir well. (Mixture will be crumbly.) Press mixture into bottom of prepared pan.

3. For topping, combine dates, pecans and water in medium saucepan. Bring to a boil. Reduce heat; simmer until mixture thickens, stirring constantly. Remove from heat. Stir in vanilla extract. Spread date mixture evenly over crust. Bake at 350°F for 25 to 30 minutes. Cool completely. Dust with confectioners' sugar.

Makes about 32 bars

Pecan Date Bars

Strawberry Streusel Squares

1 package (about 18 ounces) yellow cake mix, divided
3 tablespoons uncooked old-fashioned oats
1 tablespoon margarine
1½ cups sliced strawberries
¾ cup plus 2 tablespoons water, divided
¾ cup diced strawberries
3 egg whites
⅓ cup unsweetened applesauce
½ teaspoon ground cinnamon
⅛ teaspoon ground nutmeg

1. Preheat oven to 350°F. Spray 13×9-inch baking pan with nonstick cooking spray; lightly coat with flour.

2. Combine ½ cup cake mix and oats in small bowl. Cut in margarine until mixture resembles coarse crumbs; set aside.

3. Place 1½ cups sliced strawberries and 2 tablespoons water in blender or food processor. Process until smooth. Transfer to small bowl; stir in ¾ cup diced strawberries. Set aside.

4. Place remaining cake mix in large bowl. Add remaining ¾ cup water, egg whites, applesauce, cinnamon and nutmeg. Beat at low speed of electric mixer 30 seconds or just until moistened. Beat at medium speed 2 minutes. Pour batter into prepared pan.

5. Spoon strawberry mixture evenly over batter, spreading lightly. Sprinkle evenly with oat mixture. Bake 31 to 34 minutes or until toothpick inserted into center comes out clean. Cool completely in pan on wire rack. *Makes 12 servings*

Strawberry Streusel Squares

Lemon Crumb Bars

1 (18.25-ounce) package lemon or yellow cake mix
½ cup (1 stick) butter or margarine, softened
1 egg
2 cups finely crushed saltine cracker crumbs
3 egg yolks
1 (14-ounce) can EAGLE BRAND® Sweetened Condensed Milk
   (NOT evaporated milk)
½ cup lemon juice from concentrate

1. Preheat oven to 350°F. Grease 15×10×1-inch baking pan. In large mixing bowl, combine cake mix, butter and 1 egg; mix well. (Mixture will be crumbly.) Stir in cracker crumbs. Reserve 2 cups crumb mixture. Press remaining crumb mixture firmly on bottom of prepared pan. Bake 15 minutes.

2. Meanwhile, in medium mixing bowl, combine egg yolks, Eagle Brand and lemon juice; mix well. Spread evenly over baked crust.

3. Top with reserved crumb mixture. Bake 20 minutes or until firm. Cool. Cut into bars. Store covered in refrigerator. *Makes 3 to 4 dozen bars*

Prep Time: 30 minutes
Bake Time: 35 minutes

tip

To soften butter for use in batters and doughs, place 1 stick of butter on a microwavable plate and heat at LOW (30% power) about 30 seconds or just until softened.

Lemon Crumb Bars

Easy Turtle Squares

1 package (about 18 ounces) chocolate cake mix
½ cup butter, melted
¼ cup milk
1 cup (6 ounces) semisweet chocolate chips
1 cup chopped pecans
1 jar (12 ounces) caramel ice cream topping

1. Preheat oven to 350°F. Spray 13×9-inch baking pan with nonstick cooking spray.

2. Combine cake mix, butter and milk in large bowl. Press half of mixture into prepared pan.

3. Bake 7 to 8 minutes or until batter begins to form crust. Carefully remove from oven. Sprinkle chocolate chips and half of pecans over partially baked crust. Drizzle caramel topping over chips and pecans. Drop spoonfuls of remaining cake batter over caramel mixture; sprinkle with remaining pecans.

4. Bake additional 18 to 20 minutes or until top springs back when lightly touched with finger. (Caramel center will be soft.) Cool completely on wire rack. Cut into squares. *Makes 24 squares*

Easy Turtle Squares

Sweet Walnut Maple Bars

Crust
- **1 package DUNCAN HINES® Moist Deluxe® Classic Yellow Cake Mix, divided**
- **⅓ cup butter or margarine, melted**
- **1 egg**

Topping
- **1⅓ cups MRS. BUTTERWORTH'S® Maple Syrup**
- **3 eggs**
- **⅓ cup firmly packed light brown sugar**
- **½ teaspoon maple flavoring or vanilla extract**
- **1 cup chopped walnuts**

1. Preheat oven to 350°F. Grease 13×9×2-inch baking pan.

2. For crust, reserve ⅔ cup cake mix; set aside. Combine remaining cake mix, melted butter and egg in large bowl. Stir until thoroughly blended. (Mixture will be crumbly.) Press into prepared pan. Bake at 350°F for 15 to 20 minutes or until light golden brown.

3. For topping, combine reserved cake mix, maple syrup, eggs, brown sugar and maple flavoring in large bowl. Beat at low speed with electric mixer for 3 minutes. Pour over crust. Sprinkle with walnuts. Bake at 350°F for 30 to 35 minutes or until filling is set. Cool completely. Cut into bars. Store leftover cookie bars in refrigerator.

Makes 24 bars

Sweet Walnut Maple Bars

Chocolate Caramel Nut Bars

1 package (18¼ ounces) devil's food cake mix
¾ cup butter, melted
½ cup milk, divided
60 vanilla caramels
1 cup *each* chopped cashews and semisweet chocolate chips

Preheat oven to 350°F. Grease 13×9-inch baking pan. Mix cake mix, butter and ¼ cup milk in bowl. Spread half of batter evenly in pan. Bake 7 to 8 minutes or until batter just begins to form crust. Remove from oven. Meanwhile, cook and stir caramels and remaining ¼ cup milk in heavy saucepan over low heat 5 minutes or until mixture is smooth. Pour caramel mixture over partially baked crust; sprinkle with cashews and chocolate chips. Drop spoonfuls of remaining batter evenly on top. Bake 18 to 20 minutes or until top springs back when lightly touched with finger. (Caramel center will be soft.) Cool completely on wire rack. *Makes about 48 bars*

Pumpkin Cheesecake Bars

1 (16-ounce) package pound cake mix
3 eggs, divided
2 tablespoons butter or margarine, melted
4 teaspoons pumpkin pie spice, divided
1 (8-ounce) package cream cheese, softened
1 (14-ounce) can EAGLE BRAND® Sweetened Condensed Milk
(NOT evaporated milk)
1 (15-ounce) can pumpkin
½ teaspoon salt
1 cup chopped nuts

1. Preheat oven to 350°F. In large mixing bowl, beat cake mix, 1 egg, butter and 2 teaspoons pumpkin pie spice on low speed of electric mixer until crumbly. Press onto bottom of ungreased 15×10×1-inch jelly-roll pan.

2. In large mixing bowl, beat cream cheese until fluffy. Gradually beat in Eagle Brand until smooth. Beat in remaining 2 eggs, pumpkin, remaining 2 teaspoons pumpkin pie spice and salt; mix well. Pour over crust; sprinkle with nuts.

3. Bake 30 to 35 minutes or until set. Cool. Chill; cut into bars. Store covered in refrigerator. *Makes 4 dozen bars*

Chocolate Caramel Nut Bars

Orange Chess Bars

Crust
    1 package DUNCAN HINES® Moist Deluxe® Orange Supreme Cake Mix
    ½ cup vegetable oil
    ⅓ cup chopped pecans

Topping
    1 pound (3½ to 4 cups) confectioners' sugar
    1 package (8 ounces) cream cheese, softened
    2 eggs
    2 teaspoons grated orange peel

1. Preheat oven to 350°F. Grease 13×9-inch baking pan.

2. For crust, combine cake mix, oil and pecans in large bowl. Stir until blended. (Mixture will be crumbly.) Press in bottom of prepared pan.

3. For topping, combine confectioners' sugar and cream cheese in large bowl. Beat at low speed with electric mixer until blended. Add eggs and orange peel. Beat at low speed until blended. Pour over crust. Bake 30 to 35 minutes or until topping is set. Cool. Refrigerate until ready to serve. Cut into bars.   *Makes about 24 bars*

Cherry Spice Bars

1 (10-ounce) jar maraschino cherries
1 (18¼-ounce) package spice cake mix
¼ cup butter or margarine, melted
¼ cup firmly packed brown sugar
¼ cup water
2 eggs

Glaze
1 cup confectioners' sugar
1 tablespoon lemon juice
1 to 2 teaspoons milk

Drain maraschino cherries; discard juice or save for another use. Cut cherries in half. Combine dry cake mix, melted butter, brown sugar, water and eggs in a large mixing bowl; mix with a spoon or electric mixer until well combined and smooth. Stir in maraschino cherries. Spread batter into a greased 13×9×2-inch baking pan.

Bake in a preheated 375°F oven 20 to 25 minutes, or until top springs back when lightly touched. Let cool in pan on wire rack.

For the glaze, combine confectioners' sugar and lemon juice; add enough milk to make a thick glaze. Drizzle glaze over cake. Allow glaze to set. Cut into bars. Store, up to one week, in an airtight container with sheets of waxed paper between each layer of bars.   *Makes 2 dozen bars*

Favorite recipe from **Cherry Marketing Institute**

Apricot Crumb Squares

1 package (18¼ ounces) yellow cake mix
1 teaspoon ground cinnamon
½ teaspoon ground nutmeg
¼ cup plus 2 tablespoons cold margarine, cut into pieces
¾ cup uncooked multigrain oatmeal cereal or old-fashioned oats
1 whole egg
2 egg whites
1 tablespoon water
1 jar (10 ounces) apricot fruit spread
2 tablespoons packed light brown sugar

1. Preheat oven to 350°F. Combine cake mix, cinnamon and nutmeg in medium bowl. Cut in margarine with pastry blender or 2 knives until coarse crumbs form. Stir in cereal. Reserve 1 cup mixture. Mix egg, egg whites and water into remaining crumb mixture.

2. Spread batter evenly in ungreased 13×9-inch baking pan; top with fruit spread. Sprinkle reserved 1 cup cereal mixture over fruit spread; sprinkle with brown sugar.

3. Bake 35 to 40 minutes or until top is golden brown. Cool in pan on wire rack; cut into 15 squares. *Makes 15 servings*

Apricot Crumb Squares

delightful desserts

Cookie Pizza Cake

1 package (18 ounces) refrigerated chocolate chip cookie dough
1 package (18¼ ounces) chocolate cake mix, plus ingredients to prepare mix
1 cup prepared vanilla frosting
½ cup peanut butter
1 to 2 tablespoons milk
1 container (16 ounces) chocolate frosting
Chocolate peanut butter cups, chopped (optional)

1. Preheat oven to 350°F. Coat two 12×1-inch round pizza pans with nonstick cooking spray. Press cookie dough evenly into one pan. Bake 15 to 20 minutes or until edges are golden brown. Cool 20 minutes in pan on wire rack. Remove from pan; cool completely on wire rack.

2. Prepare cake mix according to package directions. Fill second pan ¼ to ½ full with batter. (Reserve remaining cake batter for another use, such as cupcakes.) Bake 10 to 15 minutes or until toothpick inserted into center comes out clean. Cool 15 minutes on wire rack. Gently remove cake from pan; cool completely.

3. Combine vanilla frosting and peanut butter in small bowl. Gradually stir in milk, 1 tablespoon at a time, until of spreadable consistency.

4. Place cookie on serving plate. Spread peanut butter frosting over cookie. Place cake on top of cookie, trimming cookie to match size of cake, if necessary. Frost top and side of cake with chocolate frosting. Garnish with peanut butter cups, if desired.

Makes 12 to 14 servings

Cookie Pizza Cake

Strawberry Shortcake

Cake
> **1 package DUNCAN HINES® Moist Deluxe® French Vanilla Cake Mix**
> **3 eggs**
1¼ **cups water**
> ½ **cup butter or margarine, softened**

Filling and Topping
> **2 cups whipping cream, chilled**
> ⅓ **cup sugar**
> ½ **teaspoon vanilla extract**
> **1 quart fresh strawberries, rinsed, drained and sliced**
> **Mint leaves for garnish**

1. Preheat oven to 350°F. Grease two 9-inch round cake pans with butter or margarine. Sprinkle bottoms and sides with granulated sugar.

2. For cake, combine cake mix, eggs, water and butter in large bowl. Beat at low speed with electric mixer until moistened. Beat at medium speed for 2 minutes. Pour into prepared pans. Bake at 350°F for 30 to 35 minutes or until toothpick inserted in center comes out clean. Cool in pan 10 minutes. Invert onto cooling rack. Cool completely.

3. For filling and topping, place whipping cream, sugar and vanilla extract in large bowl. Beat with electric mixer at high speed until stiff peaks form. Reserve ⅓ cup for garnish. Place one cake layer on serving plate. Spread with half of remaining whipped cream and half of sliced strawberries. Place second cake layer on top of strawberries. Spread with remaining whipped cream and top with remaining strawberries. Dollop with reserved ⅓ cup whipped cream and garnish with mint leaves. Refrigerate until ready to serve. *Makes 12 servings*

Strawberry Shortcake

Decadent Chocolate Delight

1 package (about 18 ounces) chocolate cake mix
8 ounces sour cream
1 cup chocolate chips
1 cup water
4 eggs
¾ cup vegetable oil
1 package (4-serving size) instant chocolate pudding and pie filling mix

Slow Cooker Directions

1. Lightly grease inside of slow cooker.

2. Combine all ingredients in large bowl; mix well. Pour into slow cooker. Cover; cook on LOW 6 to 8 hours or on HIGH 3 to 4 hours. Serve hot or warm with ice cream. *Makes 12 servings*

Creamy Banana Toffee Dessert

1 package DUNCAN HINES® Moist Deluxe® Butter Recipe Golden Cake Mix
1 package (4-serving size) banana cream-flavor instant pudding and pie filling mix
1½ cups milk
1 container (8 ounces) frozen non-dairy whipped topping, thawed
3 medium bananas, sliced
¾ cup English toffee bits

1. Preheat oven to 375°F. Grease and flour 10-inch tube pan.

2. Prepare, bake and cool cake as directed on package. Meanwhile, combine pudding mix and milk in medium bowl; stir until well blended. Chill 5 minutes. Fold in whipped topping. Chill while cake cools.

3. To assemble, cut cake into 12 slices. Place 6 cake slices in 3-quart clear glass bowl. Top with half of bananas, pudding and toffee bits. Repeat layering. Chill until ready to serve. *Makes 12 to 14 servings*

Decadent Chocolate Delight

Chocolate Chip Cheesecake

1 package DUNCAN HINES® Moist Deluxe® Devil's Food Cake Mix
½ cup vegetable oil
3 packages (8 ounces each) cream cheese, softened
1½ cups granulated sugar
1 cup sour cream
1½ teaspoons vanilla extract
4 eggs, lightly beaten
¾ cup mini semisweet chocolate chips, divided
1 teaspoon all-purpose flour

1. Preheat oven to 350°F. Grease 10-inch springform pan.

2. Combine cake mix and oil in large bowl. Mix well. Press onto bottom of prepared pan. Bake at 350°F for 22 to 25 minutes or until set. Remove from oven. *Increase oven temperature to 450°F.*

3. Place cream cheese in large mixing bowl. Beat at low speed with electric mixer, adding sugar gradually. Add sour cream and vanilla extract, mixing until blended. Add eggs, mixing only until incorporated. Toss ½ cup chocolate chips with flour. Fold into cream cheese mixture. Pour filling onto crust. Sprinkle with remaining ¼ cup chocolate chips. Bake at 450°F for 5 to 7 minutes. *Reduce oven temperature to 250°F.* Bake at 250°F for 60 to 65 minutes or until set. Loosen cake from side of pan with knife or metal spatula. Cool completely in pan on cooling rack. Refrigerate until ready to serve. Remove side of pan.   *Makes 12 to 16 servings*

Hint: Place pan of water on bottom rack of oven during baking to prevent cheesecake from cracking.

tip

To quickly soften cream cheese, unwrap 8 ounces of cream cheese and place on a microwavable plate. Heat at MEDIUM (50% power) 15 to 20 seconds or just until softened. Let the cream cheese stand about 1 minute before using.

Chocolate Chip Cheesecake

Deep Dish Mocha Tiramisu

1 (14-ounce) can EAGLE BRAND® Sweetened Condensed Milk (NOT evaporated milk), divided
1 (18¼-ounce) package chocolate cake mix with pudding in the mix
1 cup water
2 eggs
½ cup vegetable oil
   Creamy Coffee Filling (page 206)
   Espresso Sauce (page 206)
½ cup coffee liqueur
   Chocolate-covered coffee beans

1. Preheat oven to 350°F. Grease 5 (8-inch) round cake pans. Reserve ¼ cup Eagle Brand for Creamy Coffee Filling.

2. In large mixing bowl, beat ¾ cup Eagle Brand, cake mix, water, eggs and oil until blended. Pour 1 cup batter into each prepared pan.

3. Bake 13 to 14 minutes. Cool in pans on wire racks 10 minutes. Remove from pans; cool completely on wire racks. Prepare Creamy Coffee Filling and Espresso Sauce.

4. Brush each cake layer evenly with liqueur. Place 1 cake layer in 4-quart trifle dish or bowl; top with 1½ cups Creamy Coffee Filling. Drizzle with ½ cup Espresso Sauce. Repeat procedure with remaining cake layers, 1 cup filling, and ¼ cup sauce, ending with cake layer. Garnish with chocolate-covered coffee beans. Chill. Store covered in refrigerator. *Makes 12 servings*

Prep Time: 15 minutes
Bake Time: 13 to 14 minutes

continued on page 206

Deep Dish Mocha Tiramisu

Deep Dish Mocha Tiramisu, continued

Creamy Coffee Filling

**¼ cup reserved EAGLE BRAND® Sweetened Condensed Milk
(NOT evaporated milk)
1 (8-ounce) package cream cheese, softened
2 tablespoons coffee liqueur
1½ cups cold whipping cream**

In large mixing bowl, beat first 3 ingredients until blended, about 4 minutes. Add whipping cream and beat until stiff peaks form. Chill, if desired.

Makes 4½ cups filling

Prep Time: 10 minutes

Espresso Sauce

**1 cup water
½ cup ground espresso
1 (14-ounce) can EAGLE BRAND® Sweetened Condensed Milk
(NOT evaporated milk)
¼ cup (½ stick) butter or margarine**

In small saucepan over medium heat, bring 1 cup water and ground espresso to a boil. Remove from heat and let stand 5 minutes. Pour mixture through fine wire-mesh strainer; discard grounds. In small saucepan over medium heat, combine espresso and Eagle Brand. Bring to a boil. Remove from heat; stir in butter. Cool.

Makes 1¼ cups sauce

Prep Time: 10 minutes

Very Berry Summer Trifle

1 box white cake mix
1 ¼ cups water
⅓ cup CRISCO® Pure Vegetable Oil
3 egg whites
1 cup SMUCKER'S® Strawberry or Raspberry Jam
½ cup pineapple juice, divided
6 to 8 coconut macaroons, crushed, divided
1 quart strawberries, raspberries, blueberries or any combination of berries
2 (3- to 4-ounce) boxes vanilla pudding, prepared according to package instructions
2 cups whipped cream or whipped topping of choice
¼ cup slivered blanched almonds, toasted

1. Preheat oven to 350°F. Spray two 8-inch round baking pans with CRISCO® Cooking Spray.

2. Combine cake mix, water, oil and egg whites in large bowl. Beat on low speed 30 seconds; beat on medium speed 2 minutes, scraping bowl occasionally, or beat 2 minutes by hand, using wire whisk. Pour batter into prepared pans.

3. Bake for 25 to 30 minutes or until toothpick inserted in center comes out clean. Cool 10 minutes in pan. Run knife around side of pan before removing. Cool completely on wire rack.

4. Cut cooled cake horizontally in half. Spread bottom half with jam; replace top layer. (There will be 1 cake layer leftover to prepare as desired.)

5. Cut filled cake into bite-size pieces; arrange randomly in bottom of deep 10×4-inch bowl or trifle bowl. Sprinkle with pineapple juice. Reserve 2 tablespoons macaroons; sprinkle remaining macaroons over cake. Place single layer of berries over cake. Pour prepared pudding over berries. Sprinkle reserved crushed macaroons over berries.

6. Spoon whipped cream into pastry bag; decorate trifle. Garnish with additional berries and toasted slivered almonds. Cover with plastic wrap. Chill 6 hours or overnight before serving. *Makes 16 servings*

Chocolate Angel Food Dessert

1 package DUNCAN HINES® Angel Food Cake Mix
16 large marshmallows
½ cup milk
1 package (11 ounces) milk chocolate chips
1 pint whipping cream
¼ cup semisweet chocolate chips
1½ teaspoons shortening

1. Preheat oven to 375°F. Prepare, bake and cool cake following package directions.

2. Melt marshmallows and milk in heavy saucepan over low heat. Remove from heat; stir in milk chocolate chips until melted. Cool to room temperature. Beat whipping cream in large bowl until stiff peaks form. Fold cooled chocolate mixture into whipped cream. Refrigerate until of spreading consistency.

3. To assemble, split cake horizontally into 3 even layers. Place 1 cake layer on serving plate. Spread with one-fourth of frosting. Repeat with second layer and one-fourth of frosting. Top with third layer. Frost side and top with remaining frosting. Refrigerate.

4. For drizzle, place semisweet chocolate chips and shortening in 1-cup glass measuring cup. Microwave at MEDIUM (50% power) for 1 minute. Stir until smooth. Drizzle melted chocolate around outer top edge of cake, allowing mixture to run down side unevenly. Refrigerate until ready to serve.   *Makes 12 to 16 servings*

Punch Bowl Party Cake

1 package (18¼ ounces) chocolate cake mix, plus ingredients to prepare mix
1 package (4-serving size) instant vanilla pudding and pie filling mix, plus ingredients to prepare mix
2 cans (21 ounces each) cherry pie filling
1 cup chopped pecans
1 container (12 ounces) frozen nondairy whipped topping, thawed

Prepare cake mix and bake according to package directions for 13×9-inch cake; cool completely. Prepare pudding mix according to package directions. Crumble half of cake into punch bowl. Top with half of pudding. Reserve a few cherries from pie filling. Top pudding with pie filling, nuts and whipped topping. Repeat all layers ending with whipped topping. Garnish with reserved cherries.   *Makes 12 to 14 servings*

Chocolate Angel Food Dessert

Hot Fudge Sundae Cake

1 package DUNCAN HINES® Moist Deluxe® Dark Chocolate Fudge Cake Mix
½ gallon brick vanilla ice cream

Fudge Sauce
1 can (12 ounces) evaporated milk
1¼ cups sugar
4 squares (1 ounce each) unsweetened chocolate
¼ cup butter or margarine
1½ teaspoons vanilla extract
¼ teaspoon salt
Whipped cream and maraschino cherries for garnish

1. Preheat oven to 350°F. Grease and flour 13×9×2-inch baking pan. Prepare, bake and cool cake following package directions.

2. Remove cake from pan. Split cake in half horizontally. Place bottom layer back in pan. Cut ice cream into even slices and place evenly over bottom cake layer (use all the ice cream). Place remaining cake layer over ice cream. Cover and freeze.

3. For fudge sauce, combine evaporated milk and sugar in medium saucepan. Cook, stirring constantly, on medium heat until mixture comes to a rolling boil. Boil and stir for 1 minute. Add unsweetened chocolate and stir until melted. Beat over medium heat until smooth. Remove from heat. Stir in butter, vanilla extract and salt.

4. Cut cake into squares. For each serving, place cake square on plate; spoon hot fudge sauce on top. Garnish with whipped cream and maraschino cherry.

Makes 12 to 16 servings

Note: Fudge sauce may be prepared ahead and refrigerated in tightly sealed jar. Reheat when ready to serve.

Hot Fudge Sundae Cake

Rich Pumpkin Cheesecake

Crust
   1 package DUNCAN HINES® Moist Deluxe® Spice Cake Mix
   ½ cup butter or margarine, melted

Filling
   3 packages (8 ounces each) cream cheese, softened
   1 can (14 ounces) sweetened condensed milk
   1 can (16 ounces) solid pack pumpkin
   4 eggs
   1 tablespoon pumpkin pie spice

Topping
   1 package (2½ ounces) sliced almonds
   2 cups whipping cream, chilled
   ¼ cup sugar

1. Preheat oven to 375°F.

2. For crust, combine cake mix and melted butter in large bowl; press into bottom of *ungreased* 10-inch springform pan.

3. For filling, combine cream cheese and sweetened condensed milk in large bowl. Beat with electric mixer at high speed 2 minutes. Add pumpkin, eggs and pumpkin pie spice. Beat at high speed 1 minute. Pour over prepared crust in pan. Bake at 375°F for 65 to 70 minutes or until set. Cool completely on rack. Refrigerate 2 hours. Loosen cake from side of pan; remove side of pan.

4. For topping, preheat oven to 300°F. Toast almonds on baking sheet at 300°F for 4 to 5 minutes or until fragrant and light golden brown. Cool completely. Beat whipping cream in medium bowl with electric mixer at high speed until soft peaks form. Gradually add sugar; beat until stiff peaks form. Spread over top of chilled cake. Garnish with toasted almonds. Refrigerate until ready to serve. *Makes 8 to 12 servings*

Note: To prepare in 13×9×2-inch pan, bake at 350°F for 35 minutes or until set.

Rich Pumpkin Cheesecake

Trifle Spectacular

1 package DUNCAN HINES® Moist Deluxe® Devil's Food Cake Mix
1 can (14 ounces) sweetened condensed milk
1 cup cold water
1 package (4-serving size) vanilla-flavor instant pudding and pie
    filling mix
2 cups whipping cream, whipped
2 tablespoons orange juice
2½ cups sliced fresh strawberries
1 pint fresh raspberries
2 kiwifruit, peeled and sliced
1½ cups frozen whipped topping, thawed for garnish
    Mint leaves for garnish (optional)

1. Preheat oven to 350°F. Grease and flour two 9-inch round cake pans.

2. Prepare, bake and cool cake following package directions for basic recipe. Cut one cake layer into 1-inch cubes. Freeze remaining cake layer for another use.

3. Combine sweetened condensed milk and water in large bowl. Stir until blended. Add pudding mix. Beat until thoroughly blended. Chill 5 minutes. Fold whipped cream into pudding mixture.

4. To assemble, spread 2 cups pudding mixture into 3-quart trifle dish (or 3-quart clear glass bowl with straight sides). Arrange half the cake cubes over pudding mixture. Sprinkle with 1 tablespoon orange juice. Layer with 1 cup strawberry slices, half the raspberries and one-third of kiwifruit slices. Repeat layers. Top with remaining pudding mixture. Garnish with whipped topping, remaining ½ cup strawberry slices, kiwifruit slices and mint leaves, if desired.   *Makes 10 to 12 servings*

Hint: Since the different layers contribute to the beauty of this recipe, arrange the fruit pieces to show attractively along the sides of the trifle dish.

Trifle Spectacular

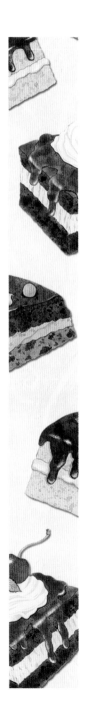

Boston Cream Pie

1 package DUNCAN HINES® Moist Deluxe® Classic Yellow Cake Mix
4 containers (3½ ounces each) ready-to-eat vanilla pudding
1 container DUNCAN HINES® Chocolate Frosting

1. Preheat oven to 350°F. Grease and flour two 8- or 9-inch round pans.

2. Prepare, bake and cool cake following package directions for basic recipe.

3. To assemble, place each cake layer on serving plate. Split layers in half horizontally. Spread contents of 2 containers of vanilla pudding on bottom layer of one cake. Place top layer on filling. Repeat for second cake layer. Remove lid and foil top of Chocolate frosting container. Heat in microwave oven at HIGH (100% power) for 25 to 30 seconds. Stir. (Mixture should be thin.) Spread half the chocolate glaze over top of each cake. Refrigerate until ready to serve.   *Makes 12 to 16 servings*

Hint: For a richer flavor, substitute Duncan Hines® Butter Recipe Golden cake mix in place of Yellow cake mix.

Pineapple Delight

1 package (18¼ ounces) pineapple cake mix, plus ingredients to
**   prepare mix**
2 packages (4-serving size) vanilla-flavored instant pudding mix
3 cups milk
1 cup powdered sugar
1 container (8 ounces) frozen whipped topping, thawed
1 can (20 ounces) pineapple chunks, drained

1. Prepare cake mix and bake according to package directions for 11×8-inch pan. Cool completely.

2. Combine pudding mix, milk, powdered sugar and whipped topping in medium bowl; set aside.

3. Crumble ½ of cake into large bowl. Top with ½ of pudding mixture. Spread ½ of pineapple over pudding mixture. Repeat layers starting with remaining cake and ending with pineapple. Refrigerate 3 to 4 hours before serving.

Makes 10 servings

Boston Cream Pie

Mini Neapolitan Ice Cream Cakes

1 package (18¼ ounces) white cake mix
¾ cup water
⅓ cup vegetable oil
3 eggs
⅓ cup unsweetened cocoa powder
4 cups slightly softened strawberry ice cream
   Unsweetened cocoa powder, powdered sugar, dark chocolate
   curls and strawberry fans for garnish

1. Preheat oven to 350°F. Grease 4 (5¾×3¼×2-inch) mini-loaf pans; set aside.

2. Combine cake mix, water, oil and eggs in large bowl. Beat at low speed of electric mixer 30 seconds or until just blended. Beat 2 minutes at medium speed or until well blended, scraping side of bowl occasionally. Reserve 1¾ cups batter. Add cocoa to remaining batter; stir until well blended.

3. Divide chocolate batter evenly between 2 prepared pans. Divide reserved plain batter evenly between remaining 2 prepared pans.

4. Bake 30 minutes or until toothpicks inserted into centers come out clean. Cool in pans 10 minutes. Remove cakes from pans to wire racks; cool completely.

5. Trim rounded tops of cakes with serrated knife; discard trimmings. Cut each cake in half horizontally. Line 4 clean mini-loaf pans with plastic wrap, leaving 2-inch overhang on all sides. Place 1 chocolate cake layer in each pan.

6. Place ice cream in large bowl; beat at medium speed about 30 seconds or just until spreadable. Spread 1 cup ice cream over each chocolate cake layer in pans; top with vanilla cake layers. Cover tops of cakes with plastic wrap. Freeze at least 4 hours.

7. Remove cakes from loaf pans. Remove plastic wrap; trim any uneven sides. Place 2 cakes vanilla side up; sprinkle lightly with cocoa powder. Place remaining 2 cakes chocolate side up; sprinkle lightly with powdered sugar. Garnish all 4 cakes with dark chocolate curls and strawberry fans. To serve, cut each cake crosswise into 3 slices.

Makes 4 cakes (12 servings)

Mini Neapolitan Ice Cream Cakes

Berry Cobbler Cake

2 cups (1 pint) fresh or frozen berries (blueberries, blackberries, and/or raspberries)
1 package (1-layer size) yellow cake mix
1 teaspoon ground cinnamon
1 egg
1 cup water, divided
¼ cup sugar
1 tablespoon cornstarch
Ice cream (optional)

1. Preheat oven to 375°F.

2. Place berries in 9-inch square baking pan. Combine cake mix and cinnamon in large bowl. Add egg and ¼ cup water; stir until well blended. Spoon over berries.

3. Combine sugar and cornstarch in small bowl. Stir in remaining ¾ cup water until sugar mixture dissolves; pour over cake batter and berries.

4. Bake 40 to 45 minutes or until lightly browned. Serve warm or at room temperature with ice cream, if desired. *Makes 6 servings*

Kahlúa® Chocolate-Mint Trifle

1 chocolate cake mix (without pudding), plus ingredients to prepare mix
1 cup KAHLÚA® Liqueur
2 boxes (4-serving size) instant chocolate pudding mix
3½ cups milk
3 cups whipped topping
Peppermint candy, crushed

Prepare, bake and cool cake in 13×9-inch baking pan according to package directions. Poke holes in cake with fork; pour Kahlúa® over top. Refrigerate overnight. Cut cake into cubes.

Prepare pudding mix with milk in large bowl according to package directions. In large clear glass trifle dish or glass bowl, layer ⅓ each of cake cubes, pudding, whipped topping and candy. Repeat layers two more times. Refrigerate leftovers.

Makes about 18 servings

Berry Cobbler Cake

Pumpkin Pie Crunch

1 can (16 ounces) solid pack pumpkin
1 can (12 ounces) evaporated milk
3 eggs
1½ cups sugar
4 teaspoons pumpkin pie spice
½ teaspoon salt
1 package DUNCAN HINES® Moist Deluxe® Classic Yellow Cake Mix
1 cup chopped pecans
1 cup butter or margarine, melted
Whipped topping

1. Preheat oven to 350°F. Grease bottom only of 13×9×2-inch pan.

2. Combine pumpkin, evaporated milk, eggs, sugar, pumpkin pie spice and salt in large bowl. Pour into prepared pan. Sprinkle dry cake mix evenly over pumpkin mixture. Top with pecans. Drizzle with melted butter. Bake at 350°F for 50 to 55 minutes or until golden. Cool completely. Serve with whipped topping. Refrigerate leftovers.

Makes 16 to 20 servings

Hint: For a richer flavor, try using Duncan Hines® Moist Deluxe® Butter Recipe Golden Cake Mix.

Pumpkin Pie Crunch

Rum and Spumone Layered Torte

1 package (18¼ ounces) butter recipe yellow cake mix
3 eggs
½ cup butter, softened
⅓ cup plus 2 teaspoons rum, divided
⅓ cup water
1 quart spumone ice cream, softened
1 cup cold whipping cream
1 tablespoon powdered sugar
Candied cherries
Red and green sugars for decorating (optional)

1. Preheat oven to 375°F. Grease and flour 15½×10½×1-inch jelly-roll pan. Combine cake mix, eggs, butter, ⅓ cup rum and water in large bowl. Beat with electric mixer at low speed until moistened. Beat at high speed 4 minutes. Pour evenly into prepared pan.

2. Bake 20 to 25 minutes or until toothpick inserted in center comes out clean. Cool in pan 10 minutes. Turn out of pan onto wire rack; cool completely.

3. Cut cake into three 10×5-inch pieces. Place one cake layer on serving plate. Spread with half the softened ice cream. Cover with second cake layer. Spread with remaining ice cream. Place remaining cake layer on top. Gently push down. Wrap cake in plastic wrap and freeze at least 4 hours.

4. Just before serving, combine cream, powdered sugar and remaining 2 teaspoons rum in small chilled bowl. Beat with chilled beaters at high speed until stiff peaks form. Remove cake from freezer. Spread thin layer of whipped cream mixture over top of cake. Place star tip in pastry bag; fill with remaining whipped cream mixture. Pipe rosettes around outer top edges of cake. Place candied cherries in narrow strip down center of cake. Sprinkle colored sugars over rosettes, if desired. Serve immediately.

Makes 8 to 10 servings

Rum and Spumone Layered Torte

special occasions

Chocolate-Raspberry Layer Cake

**2 packages (about 18 ounces each) chocolate cake mix, plus
    ingredients to prepare mixes**
1 jar (10 ounces) seedless red raspberry fruit spread
1 package (12 ounces) white chocolate chips, divided
1 container (16 ounces) chocolate frosting
½ pint fresh raspberries
1 to 2 cups toasted sliced almonds

1. Preheat oven to 350°F. Grease and flour 4 (9-inch) round cake pans. Prepare cake mixes according to package directions. Pour into prepared pans. Bake as directed on package. Cool completely.

2. Place one cake layer on serving plate. Spread with ⅓ of fruit spread. Sprinkle with ½ cup white chocolate chips. Repeat with second and third cake layers, fruit spread and white chocolate chips.

3. Place fourth cake layer on top. Frost top and side of cake with chocolate frosting. Decorate cake in alternating concentric circles of raspberries and remaining ½ cup white chocolate chips. Press almonds into frosting on side of cake.

Makes 8 to 10 servings

Chocolate-Raspberry Layer Cake

Sunny Day Cake

Cake
> **1 package (18¼ ounces) white cake mix, plus ingredients to prepare mix**
> **Juice and grated peel of 1 large orange (about ½ cup juice)**

Frosting
> **2 packages (8 ounces each) cream cheese, softened**
> **½ cup milk**
> **2 teaspoons vanilla**
> **1 cup powdered sugar**

Garnish
> **1 quart strawberries washed, hulled and sliced**
> **1 orange, sliced**
> **Mint leaves (optional)**

1. Grease and flour 9-inch springform pan. Prepare cake mix according to package directions, substituting orange juice for ½ cup of liquid in directions. Stir in orange peel. Pour batter into prepared pan. Bake according to package directions. Cool completely in pan on wire rack.

2. For frosting, combine cream cheese, milk and vanilla in medium bowl. Beat at low speed of electric mixer until well blended. Add powdered sugar; beat until smooth. Cover with plastic wrap; refrigerate.

3. Remove side of springform pan; place cake (on pan bottom) on serving plate. Frost entire cake with frosting. Create cross-hatch pattern in frosting, if desired. Arrange strawberry slices and orange slices decoratively on top of cake. Loosely wrap cake with plastic wrap and refrigerate until ready to serve.   *Makes 12 servings*

Sunny Day Cake

Chocolate Cherry Torte

1 package DUNCAN HINES® Moist Deluxe® Devil's Food Cake Mix
1 can (21 ounces) cherry pie filling
¼ teaspoon almond extract
1 container (8 ounces) frozen whipped topping, thawed
¼ cup toasted sliced almonds, for garnish (see Hint)

1. Preheat oven to 350°F. Grease and flour two 9-inch round cake pans.

2. Prepare, bake and cool cake following package directions for basic recipe. Combine cherry pie filling and almond extract in small bowl. Stir until blended.

3. To assemble, place one cake layer on serving plate. Spread with 1 cup whipped topping, then half the cherry pie filling mixture. Top with second cake layer. Spread remaining pie filling to within 1½ inches of cake edge. Decorate cake edge with remaining whipped topping. Garnish with sliced almonds.

Makes 12 to 16 servings

Hint: To toast almonds, spread in a single layer on baking sheet. Bake at 325°F 4 to 6 minutes or until fragrant and golden.

Strawberry Celebration Cake

1 package DUNCAN HINES® Moist Deluxe® Strawberry Supreme Cake Mix
1 cup strawberry preserves, heated
1 container DUNCAN HINES® Creamy Home-Style Cream Cheese Frosting
Strawberry halves for garnish
Mint leaves for garnish

1. Preheat oven to 350°F. Grease and flour 10-inch Bundt or tube pan.

2. Prepare, bake and cool cake following package directions for basic recipe.

3. Split cake horizontally into three even layers. Place bottom cake layer on serving plate. Spread with ½ cup warm preserves. Repeat layering. Top with remaining cake layer. Frost cake with Cream Cheese frosting. Garnish with strawberry halves and mint leaves. Refrigerate until ready to serve. *Makes 12 to 16 servings*

Chocolate Cherry Torte

Cool and Minty Party Cake

1 (14-ounce) can EAGLE BRAND® Sweetened Condensed Milk (NOT evaporated milk)
2 teaspoons peppermint extract
8 drops green food coloring, if desired
2 cups (1 pint) whipping cream, whipped (do not use non-dairy topping)
1 (18.25- or 18.5-ounce) package white cake mix
Green crème de menthe liqueur
1 (8-ounce) container frozen non-dairy whipped topping, thawed

1. Line 9-inch round layer cake pan with aluminum foil. In large mixing bowl, combine Eagle Brand, peppermint extract and food coloring, if desired. Fold in whipped cream. Pour into prepared pan; cover. Freeze at least 6 hours or until firm.

2. Meanwhile, prepare and bake cake mix as package directs for two 9-inch round layers. Remove from pans; cool completely.

3. With fork, poke holes in cake layers, 1 inch apart, halfway through each layer. Spoon small amounts of liqueur into holes. Place one cake layer on serving plate; top with frozen Eagle Brand mixture, then second cake layer. Trim frozen layer to edge of cake layers.

4. Frost quickly with whipped topping. Return to freezer at least 6 hours before serving. Garnish as desired. Freeze leftovers. *Makes one 9-inch cake*

Cool and Minty Party Cake

Piña Colada Cake

Cake
    1 package (18¼ ounces) white cake mix, plus ingredients to
        prepare mix

Rum Filling
    ½ cup cold whipping cream
    ¼ cup dark rum
    2 tablespoons powdered sugar
    ¾ teaspoon vanilla

Whipped Topping
    2 cups cold whipping cream
    ¾ cup powdered sugar
    2 teaspoons vanilla

Garnishes
    1 fresh pineapple, peeled, cut in half lengthwise and cored
    2 cups sweetened shredded coconut, toasted*

To toast coconut, spread evenly on ungreased cookie sheet. Bake in preheated 350°F oven 5 to 7 minutes, stirring occasionally, until light golden brown.

1. Prepare cake mix and bake according to package directions using 2 (9-inch) round cake pans. Cool in pans on wire racks 15 minutes. Remove cakes from pans; cool.

2. For rum filling, combine all ingredients in small bowl until well blended. Cover with plastic wrap; refrigerate until ready to use.

3. For whipped topping, place 2 cups whipping cream in large bowl; beat 1½ to 2 minutes or until soft peaks form. Add powdered sugar and vanilla; beat 20 seconds or until stiff peaks form. Cover with plastic wrap; refrigerate until ready to use.

4. Place pineapple cut side down on cutting board; slice very thinly. Place slices on paper towels; pat dry.

5. Place 1 cake layer on serving plate. Spread half of rum filling over cake. Spread 1 cup whipped topping over filling. Sprinkle with 1 cup coconut; top with remaining cake layer. Spread remaining rum filling over cake. Spread remaining whipped topping evenly over top and side of cake; sprinkle top with remaining coconut.

6. Press pineapple slices around side of cake vertically, overlapping slightly. Reserve any remaining pineapple slices for another use. Refrigerate cake until ready to serve.

Makes 12 servings

Piña Colada Cake

Easy Cream Cake

1 package DUNCAN HINES® Moist Deluxe® Classic White Cake Mix
3 egg whites
1⅓ cups half-and-half
2 tablespoons vegetable oil
1 cup flaked coconut, finely chopped
½ cup finely chopped pecans
2 containers DUNCAN HINES® Creamy Home-Style Cream Cheese Frosting

1. Preheat oven to 350°F. Grease and flour three 8-inch round cake pans.

2. Combine cake mix, egg whites, half-and-half, oil, coconut and pecans in large bowl. Beat at low speed with electric mixer until moistened. Beat at medium speed 2 minutes. Pour into prepared pans. Bake at 350°F for 22 to 25 minutes or until toothpick inserted in center comes out clean. Cool following package directions.

3. To assemble, place one cake layer on serving plate. Spread with ¾ cup Cream Cheese frosting. Place second cake layer on top. Spread with ¾ cup frosting. Top with third layer. Spread ¾ cup frosting on top only. Garnish as desired.

Makes 12 to 16 servings

Hint: Spread leftover frosting between graham crackers for an easy snack.

Easy Cream Cake

Elegant Chocolate Angel Torte

⅓ cup HERSHEY'S Cocoa
1 package (about 16 ounces) angel food cake mix
2 envelopes (1.3 ounces each) dry whipped topping mix
1 cup cold nonfat milk
1 teaspoon vanilla extract
1 cup strawberry purée*
Strawberries

*Mash 2 cups sliced fresh strawberries (or frozen berries, thawed) in blender or food processor. Cover; blend until smooth. Purée should measure 1 cup.

1. Move oven rack to lowest position.

2. Sift cocoa over dry cake mix in large bowl; stir to blend. Proceed with mixing cake as directed on package. Bake and cool as directed for 10-inch tube pan. Carefully run knife along side of pan to loosen cake; remove from pan. Using serrated knife, slice cake horizontally into four layers.

3. Prepare whipped topping mix as directed on package, using 1 cup nonfat milk and 1 teaspoon vanilla. Fold in strawberry purée.

4. Place bottom cake layer on serving plate; spread with ¼ of strawberry topping. Set next cake layer on top; spread with ¼ of topping. Continue layering cake and topping. Garnish with strawberries. Refrigerate until ready to serve. Slice cake with sharp serrated knife, cutting with gentle sawing motion. Cover; refrigerate leftover cake.

Makes about 16 servings

Prep Time: 30 minutes
Bake Time: 45 minutes
Cool Time: 2 hours

Elegant Chocolate Angel Torte

Chocolate Petits Fours

**1 package DUNCAN HINES® Moist Deluxe® Dark Chocolate Fudge
   Cake Mix**
1 package (7 ounces) pure almond paste
½ cup seedless red raspberry jam
3 cups semisweet chocolate chips
½ cup vegetable shortening plus additional for greasing

1. Preheat oven to 350°F. Grease and flour 13×9×2-inch baking pan.

2. Prepare, bake and cool cake following package directions for basic recipe. Remove from pan. Cover and store overnight (see Hint). Level top of cake. Trim ¼-inch strip of cake from all sides. (Be careful to make straight cuts.) Cut cake into small squares, rectangles or triangles with serrated knife. Cut round and heart shapes with 1½- to 2-inch cookie cutters. Split each individual cake horizontally into two layers.

3. For filling, cut almond paste in half. Roll half the paste between two sheets of waxed paper to ⅛-inch thickness. Cut into same shapes as individual cakes. Repeat with second half of paste. Warm jam in small saucepan over low heat until thin. Remove top of one cake. Spread ¼ to ½ teaspoon jam on inside of each cut surface. Place one almond paste cutout on bottom layer. Top with second half of cake, jam side down. Repeat with remaining cakes.

4. For glaze, place chocolate chips and ½ cup shortening in 4-cup glass measuring cup. Microwave at MEDIUM (50% power) for 2 minutes; stir. Microwave for 2 minutes longer at MEDIUM; stir until smooth. Place 3 assembled cakes on cooling rack over bowl. Spoon chocolate glaze over each cake until top and sides are completely covered. Remove to waxed paper when glaze has stopped dripping. Repeat process until all cakes are covered. (Return chocolate glaze in bowl to glass measuring cup as needed; microwave at MEDIUM for 30 to 60 seconds to thin.)

5. Place remaining chocolate glaze in resealable plastic bag; seal. Place bag in bowl of hot water for several minutes. Dry with paper towel. Knead until chocolate is smooth. Snip pinpoint hole in bottom corner of bag. Drizzle or decorate top of each petit four. Let stand until chocolate is set. Store in single layer in airtight containers.

Makes 24 to 32 servings

Hint: To make cutting the cake into shapes easier, bake the cake one day before assembling.

Chocolate Petits Fours

Josephine's Tea Cakes

1 package (18¼ ounces) yellow pudding-in-the-mix cake mix, plus ingredients to prepare mix
2 cups sifted powdered sugar, divided
8 tablespoons (1 stick) unsalted butter, melted and divided
8 teaspoons milk, divided
Sugared Flowers and Fruits (recipe follows)

1. Prepare cake mix according to package directions. Bake in 10-inch square pan according to directions, allowing additional time as necessary. Cool completely.

2. Set wire rack on large baking sheet. Remove cake from pan; place on cutting board. Cut cake into 1-inch squares; place on wire rack.

3. Combine 1 cup powdered sugar and 4 tablespoons melted butter in medium bowl; stir until blended. Add 4 teaspoons milk; stir until smooth. Working quickly, drizzle glaze over half of cake squares, allowing it to drip down sides. Repeat with remaining powdered sugar, butter and milk; drizzle over remaining cake squares.

4. Prepare Sugared Flowers and Fruits. Top glazed cake squares with dry fruit and flowers before serving. *Makes 10 tea cakes*

Sugared Flowers and Fruits

Assorted edible flowers
Assorted small fruits (blueberries, raspberries, currants, kiwi pieces, kumquat slices)
1 pasteurized egg white
Granulated sugar

Brush flower petals and fruit with egg white. Sprinkle generously with sugar; set on wire rack to dry. Use to decorate cakes.

Hint: You can make these crowd-pleasing tea cakes even if you don't have time to bake a cake! Just cut a frozen or store-bought pound cake into 1-inch squares and decorate as directed.

Josephine's Tea Cakes

Double Berry Layer Cake

**1 package DUNCAN HINES® Moist Deluxe® Strawberry Supreme
Cake Mix**
⅔ cup strawberry jam
2½ cups fresh blueberries, rinsed, drained
**1 container (8 ounces) frozen whipped topping, thawed
Fresh strawberry slices for garnish**

1. Preheat oven to 350°F. Grease and flour two 9-inch round cake pans.

2. Prepare, bake and cool cake following package directions for basic recipe.

3. Place one cake layer on serving plate. Spread with ⅓ cup strawberry jam. Arrange 1 cup blueberries on jam. Spread half the whipped topping to within ½ inch of cake edge. Place second cake layer on top. Repeat with remaining ⅓ cup strawberry jam, 1 cup blueberries and remaining whipped topping. Garnish with strawberry slices and remaining ½ cup blueberries. Refrigerate until ready to serve.   *Makes 12 servings*

Hint: For best results, cut cake with serrated knife; clean knife after each slice.

tip

When selecting blueberries, look for plump, fresh berries of good blue color with a silvery bloom. Avoid shriveled blueberries or berries with a green or red tint (an indication of an underripe berry). If packaged in plastic, fresh blueberries should be stored in the refrigerator in their original package. If packaged in cardboard, the blueberries should be transferred to an airtight container. Fresh berries may be kept up to ten days. Wash them just before using.

Double Berry Layer Cake

Fall Harvest Spice Cake

1 package (18¼ ounces) spice or carrot cake mix
1 cup water
3 eggs
⅓ cup vegetable oil
⅓ cup apple butter
   Maple Buttercream Frosting (recipe follows)
2 cups coarsely chopped walnuts
¼ cup semisweet chocolate chips
¼ cup chopped almonds
2 tablespoons chopped dried apricots
2 tablespoons chopped dried cranberries*
2 tablespoons raisins

If dried cranberries are unavailable, use additional chopped dried apricots and raisins.

1. Preheat oven to 375°F. Grease and flour two 9-inch round baking pans.

2. Combine cake mix, water, eggs, oil and apple butter in medium bowl. Beat at low speed of electric mixer until blended; beat at medium speed 2 minutes. Pour batter into prepared pans.

3. Bake 35 to 40 minutes or until toothpicks inserted into centers come out clean. Let cool in pans on wire racks 10 minutes. Remove from pans; cool completely.

4. Prepare Maple Buttercream Frosting.

5. Place 1 cake layer on serving plate; frost top with Maple Buttercream Frosting. Top with second cake layer; frost top and side with frosting. Press walnuts onto side of cake.

6. Place chocolate chips in small resealable plastic food storage bag; seal. Microwave at HIGH 30 seconds; knead bag lightly. Microwave at HIGH for additional 30-second intervals until chips are completely melted, kneading bag after each 30-second interval. Cut off very tiny corner of bag. Pipe chocolate onto cake for tree trunk. Combine almonds, apricots, cranberries and raisins. Sprinkle above and below trunk to make leaves.   *Makes 12 servings*

Maple Buttercream Frosting: Beat ¼ cup softened butter and ¼ cup maple syrup in medium bowl until well blended. Gradually beat in 3 cups powdered sugar until smooth. Makes about 3 cups frosting.

Fall Harvest Spice Cake

Nutty Toffee Ice Cream Cake

1 package (18¼ ounces) devil's food cake mix, plus ingredients to
prepare mix
2 quarts vanilla ice cream, slightly softened
1½ cups toffee baking pieces, divided
1 container (14 ounces) cream-filled pirouette cookies (about
30 cookies)
1 container (16 ounces) chocolate frosting
¾ cup unsalted peanuts or nut topping, toasted and chopped
Ribbon (optional)

1. Prepare and bake cake mix in two 9-inch round cake pans coated with nonstick cooking spray according to package directions. Cool in pans on wire racks 15 minutes. Remove from pans; cool completely on wire racks.

2. Place 1 cake layer on serving plate. Spread 4 cups softened ice cream evenly over cake. Sprinkle with ¾ cup toffee pieces. Top with remaining cake layer. Spread remaining 4 cups ice cream evenly over cake. Wrap with plastic wrap coated with nonstick cooking spray; freeze about 30 minutes.

3. Meanwhile, carefully cut each cookie in half lengthwise with sharp serrated knife.

4. Remove cake from freezer. Frost side only with chocolate frosting. Place cookie halves vertically around side of cake. Sprinkle nuts and remaining ¾ cup toffee pieces over top of cake. Wrap with plastic wrap; freeze overnight or at least 8 hours until very firm. Tie ribbon around cake before serving, if desired.   *Makes 12 servings*

Nutty Toffee Ice Cream Cake

Chocolate Dream Torte

1 package DUNCAN HINES® Moist Deluxe® Dark Chocolate Fudge Cake Mix
1 (6-ounce) package semisweet chocolate chips, melted
1 (8-ounce) container frozen non-dairy whipped topping, thawed
1 container DUNCAN HINES® Creamy Home-Style Milk Chocolate Frosting
3 tablespoons finely chopped dry roasted pistachios

1. Preheat oven to 350°F. Grease and flour two 9-inch round cake pans.

2. Prepare, bake and cool cake as directed on package for basic recipe.

3. For chocolate hearts garnish, spread melted chocolate to ⅛-inch thickness on waxed paper-lined baking sheet. Cut shapes with heart cookie cutter when chocolate begins to set. Refrigerate until firm. Push out heart shapes. Set aside.

4. To assemble, split each cake layer in half horizontally. Place one split cake layer on serving plate. Spread one-third of whipped topping on top. Repeat with remaining layers and whipped topping, leaving top plain. Frost side and top with frosting. Sprinkle pistachios on top. Position chocolate hearts by pushing points down into cake. Refrigerate until ready to serve. *Makes 12 to 16 servings*

Chocolate Strawberry Dream Torte: Omit semisweet chocolate chips and chopped pistachios. Proceed as directed through step 2. Fold 1½ cups chopped fresh strawberries into whipped topping in large bowl. Assemble as directed, filling torte with strawberry mixture and frosting with Milk Chocolate frosting. Garnish cake with strawberry fans and mint leaves, if desired.

Chocolate Dream Torte

Celebration Pumpkin Cake

1 package (18¼ ounces) spice cake mix
1 can (about 16 ounces) solid-pack pumpkin
3 eggs
¼ cup butter, softened
1½ containers (16 ounces each) cream cheese frosting
⅓ cup caramel ice cream topping
Pecan halves for garnish

1. Preheat oven to 350°F. Grease and flour 3 (9-inch) round cake pans. Combine cake mix, pumpkin, eggs and butter in large bowl; beat with electric mixer at medium speed 2 minutes. Divide batter evenly among prepared pans. Bake 20 to 25 minutes or until toothpicks inserted into centers come out clean. Cool 5 minutes on wire racks; remove from pans and cool completely.

2. Place one cake layer on serving plate; cover with frosting. Repeat layers, ending with frosting. Frost side of cake. Spread caramel topping over top of cake, letting some caramel drip down side. Garnish with pecan halves.   *Makes 16 servings*

Strawberry Vanilla Cake

1 package DUNCAN HINES® Moist Deluxe® French Vanilla Cake Mix
1 container DUNCAN HINES® Creamy Home-Style Classic Vanilla
**   Frosting, divided**
⅓ cup seedless strawberry jam
Fresh strawberries for garnish (optional)

1. Preheat oven to 350°F. Grease and flour two 8- or 9-inch round cake pans.

2. Prepare, bake and cool cake following package directions for basic recipe.

3. To assemble, place one cake layer on serving plate. Place ¼ cup Vanilla frosting in small resealable plastic bag. Snip off one corner. Pipe bead of frosting on top of layer around outer edge. Fill remaining area with strawberry jam. Top with second cake layer. Spread remaining frosting on side and top of cake. Decorate with fresh strawberries, if desired.   *Makes 12 to 16 servings*

Celebration Pumpkin Cake

Pretty Package Cake

1 package (18¼ ounces) lemon cake mix, plus ingredients to prepare mix
1 container (16 ounces) lemon frosting

Ribbon
1 cup marshmallow creme
2 cups powdered sugar, sifted
Red food coloring

Cookie Garnish (optional)
1 package (18 ounces) refrigerated sugar cookie dough
Colored decorator icings

1. Prepare cake mix and bake in two 8-inch square baking pans according to package directions. Cool completely in pans on wire racks. Remove from pans. Fill and frost cake layers with lemon frosting.

2. For ribbon, combine marshmallow creme and sifted powdered sugar in medium bowl; stir until blended. Knead by hand until mixture comes together into stiff, workable dough. (Sprinkle sifted powdered sugar on hands often to keep dough from sticking.) Knead in 2 or 3 drops food coloring until desired color is reached. Roll dough to ¼-inch thickness, sprinkling with sifted powdered sugar as necessary to keep dough from sticking. Cut dough into 1½-inch-wide strips. Place strips over frosted cake to form ribbon and bow; trim ends.

3. For cookie garnish, if desired, prepare and bake 2-inch round cookies according to cookie dough package directions. Cool on wire rack. Pipe flowers onto cooled cookies in assorted colors using decorator icing. Garnish cake with cookies.

Makes 12 to 16 servings

Pretty Package Cake

Toasted Almond Supreme

1 package (18¼ ounces) devil's food cake mix, plus ingredients to prepare mix
1¼ cups strong coffee
2 cups cold whipping cream
¾ cup powdered sugar
2 tablespoons unsweetened cocoa powder
1½ teaspoons vanilla
½ cup seedless red raspberry jam
1 cup sliced almonds, toasted*
Fresh raspberries for garnish (optional)

*To toast almonds, spread in single layer on baking sheet. Bake in preheated 350°F oven 7 to 9 minutes or until golden brown, stirring frequently.

1. Lightly grease 2 (9-inch) round cake pans. Line bottoms of pans with waxed paper. Prepare cake mix according to package directions, substituting coffee for 1¼ cups liquid called for in directions. Divide batter evenly between prepared pans. Bake as directed. Cool in pans on wire racks 15 minutes. Remove from pans; cool completely on wire racks.

2. For chocolate whipped cream, place whipping cream in medium bowl; beat at high speed of electric mixer 1½ to 2 minutes or until soft peaks form. Add sugar, cocoa and vanilla; beat 15 to 20 seconds or until stiff peaks form. Cover with plastic wrap; refrigerate until ready to use.

3. Place 1 cake layer on serving plate. Stir raspberry jam until smooth. Spread half of jam over cake layer. Place remaining cake layer on top; spread remaining jam over cake layer. Frost cake with chocolate whipped cream.

4. Sprinkle half of almonds evenly over top of cake; press remaining almonds onto side of cake. Wrap loosely with plastic wrap; refrigerate until ready to serve. Just before serving, garnish with fresh raspberries, if desired.   *Makes 12 servings*

Toasted Almond Supreme

Delicate White Chocolate Cake

1 package DUNCAN HINES® Moist Deluxe® White Cake Mix
1 package (4-serving size) vanilla-flavor instant pudding and pie
   filling mix
4 egg whites
1 cup water
½ cup vegetable oil
5 ounces finely chopped white chocolate
1 cup cherry preserves
8 drops red food coloring (optional)
2 cups whipping cream, chilled
2 tablespoons confectioners' sugar
   Maraschino cherries for garnish
1 ounce white chocolate shavings for garnish

1. Preheat oven to 350°F. Cut waxed paper circles to fit bottoms of three 9-inch round cake pans. Grease bottoms and sides of pans. Line with waxed paper circles.

2. Combine cake mix, pudding mix, egg whites, water and oil in large mixing bowl. Beat at medium speed with electric mixer for 2 minutes. Fold in chopped white chocolate. Pour into prepared pans. Bake at 350°F for 18 to 22 minutes or until toothpick inserted in center comes out clean. Cool in pans 15 minutes. Invert onto cooling racks. Peel off waxed paper. Cool completely.

3. Combine cherry preserves and food coloring, if desired. Stir to blend color.

4. Beat whipping cream in large bowl until soft peaks form. Add sugar gradually. Beat until stiff peaks form.

5. To assemble, place one cake layer on serving plate. Spread ½ cup cherry preserves over cake. Place second cake layer on top. Spread with remaining preserves. Place third cake layer on top. Frost side and top of cake with whipped cream. Decorate with maraschino cherries and white chocolate shavings. Refrigerate until ready to serve. *Makes 12 to 16 servings*

Delicate White Chocolate Cake

Gems & Jewels Cake

**3 packages (about 18 ounces each) lemon cake mix, plus
    ingredients to prepare mixes
3 containers (16 ounces each) white frosting
9 drops lemon extract
    Yellow food coloring
1 package (3.4 ounces) instant lemon pudding and pie filling mix
1¾ cups milk
    Assorted candies for decoration**

1. Prepare cake mixes according to package directions. Divide batter among 3 cake pans: one 10×2-inch round, one 8×3-inch round and one 6×2-inch round. Bake according to directions, allowing additional time for larger cakes to bake completely. Cool in pans on wire racks 15 minutes. Remove from pans; cool completely on wire racks.

2. Combine frosting, lemon extract and food coloring in large bowl; stir until well blended. Prepare pudding mix according to package directions using 1¾ cups milk.

3. Trim tops of 2 largest cakes so tops are flat. Leave smallest cake layer slightly rounded. Cut each cake in half horizontally to make 2 layers. Spread ⅓ of pudding on bottom half of each cake; replace top cake layers.

4. Place largest filled cake on large serving platter. Frost entire cake. Top with medium cake; frost entire cake. Top with smallest cake; frost entire cake.

5. Decorate tiered cake with assorted candies as desired.

Makes 20 to 25 servings

Hint: To hold tiers steady, insert a long wooden skewer through the center of the cake before decorating. Or place round cake boards between the layers. Cut and serve cake one tier at a time.

Gems & Jewels Cake

Apple Cider Cake

Marzipan (recipe follows)
Red, yellow and green food colorings
1 package (18¼ ounces) spice cake mix
1¼ cups apple cider
⅓ cup vegetable oil
3 eggs
Apple Cider Filling (recipe follows)
Apple Cider Frosting (recipe follows)
2 cups coarsely chopped walnuts
Whole cloves

1. Prepare Marzipan. Divide into thirds; place each part in separate small bowl. Tint 1 bowl of marzipan with red food coloring, another bowl with yellow food coloring and remaining bowl of marzipan with green food coloring; cover and set aside.

2. Preheat oven to 350°F. Grease and flour two 9-inch round baking pans.

3. Combine cake mix, apple cider, oil and eggs in medium bowl. Beat at low speed of electric mixer until blended; beat at medium speed 2 minutes. Pour batter evenly into prepared pans.

4. Bake 30 to 35 minutes or until toothpicks inserted into centers come out clean. Let cool in pans on wire racks 10 minutes. Remove to wire racks; cool completely.

5. Prepare Apple Cider Filling and Apple Cider Frosting. Place 1 cake layer on serving plate; top with Apple Cider Filling. Top with second cake layer; frost top and side of cake with Apple Cider Frosting. Press nuts into frosting on side of cake.

6. Form red and yellow Marzipan into apple shapes. Place cloves in tops of apples for stems. Roll out green Marzipan to ¼-inch thickness; cut out leaf shapes as desired. Arrange on top and around side of cake. *Makes 12 servings*

Marzipan

1 can (8 ounces) almond paste
1 egg white*
3 cups powdered sugar

Use only grade A clean, uncracked egg.

Combine almond paste and egg white in small bowl. Add 2 cups powdered sugar; mix well. Knead in remaining 1 cup sugar until smooth and pliable. Wrap tightly in plastic wrap; refrigerate until ready to serve.   *Makes about 2 cups marzipan*

Apple Cider Filling

⅓ cup sugar
3 tablespoons cornstarch
⅔ cup apple cider
½ cup apple butter
2 tablespoons lemon juice
2 tablespoons butter or margarine

Combine sugar and cornstarch in small saucepan. Stir in apple cider and apple butter; cook over medium heat, stirring constantly, until thickened. Remove from heat; stir in lemon juice and butter. Cool completely.   *Makes about 1¼ cups filling*

Apple Cider Frosting

½ cup butter or margarine, softened
¼ cup apple cider
4 cups (about 1 pound) powdered sugar

Beat butter and apple cider in medium bowl until creamy and well blended. Gradually beat in powdered sugar until smooth.   *Makes about 4 cups frosting*

Carrot Layer Cake

Cake
- **1 package DUNCAN HINES® Moist Deluxe® Classic Yellow Cake Mix**
- **4 eggs**
- **½ cup vegetable oil**
- **3 cups grated carrots**
- **1 cup finely chopped nuts**
- **2 teaspoons ground cinnamon**

Cream Cheese Frosting
- **1 package (8 ounces) cream cheese, softened**
- **¼ cup butter or margarine, softened**
- **2 teaspoons vanilla extract**
- **4 cups confectioners' sugar**

1. Preheat oven to 350°F. Grease and flour two 8- or 9-inch round baking pans.

2. For cake, combine cake mix, eggs, oil, carrots, nuts and cinnamon in large bowl. Beat at low speed with electric mixer until moistened. Beat at medium speed for 2 minutes. Pour into prepared pans. Bake at 350°F for 35 to 40 minutes or until toothpick inserted in centers comes out clean. Cool.

3. For cream cheese frosting, place cream cheese, butter and vanilla extract in large bowl. Beat at low speed until smooth and creamy. Add confectioners' sugar gradually, beating until smooth. Add more sugar to thicken, or milk or water to thin frosting, as needed. Fill and frost cooled cake. Garnish with whole pecans.

Makes 12 to 16 servings

Carrot Layer Cake

holiday treats

I Think You're "Marbleous" Cupcakes

1 package (18¼ ounces) pudding-in-the-mix cake mix (any flavor)
1¼ cups water
3 eggs
¼ cup vegetable oil
1 container (16 ounces) vanilla frosting
1 tube (4¼ ounces) red decorating icing
Decorating tips to fit tube of icing

1. Preheat oven to 350°F. Grease or paper-line 24 (2½-inch) muffin pan cups.

2. Prepare cake mix according to package directions with water, eggs and oil. Spoon batter into prepared pans, filling each ⅔ full.

3. Bake 20 to 25 minutes or until toothpicks inserted into centers come out clean. Cool in pans 20 minutes. Remove to wire racks; cool completely.

4. Spread 1½ to 2 tablespoons frosting over each cupcake. Fit round tip onto tube of icing. Squeeze 4 to 5 dots icing over each cupcake. Swirl toothpick through icing and frosting in continuous motion to make marbleized pattern or heart shapes.

Makes about 2 dozen cupcakes

I Think You're "Marbleous" Cupcakes

Shower Them with Kisses Cake

2 packages (18¼ ounces each) white cake mix, divided
2½ cups water, divided
⅔ cup vegetable oil, divided
4 eggs
½ cup sugar, divided
¼ cup HERSHEY'S Cocoa, divided
   Premier White Buttercream Frosting (page 270)
   Chocolate Buttercream Frosting (page 270)
2 packages (10 ounces each) HERSHEY'S MINI KISSES™ Milk
   Chocolate or Semi-Sweet Chocolates
   Milk Chocolate Filigree Hearts (page 271)

1. Heat oven to 350°F. Grease and flour 8-inch square baking pan and 8-inch round baking pan. Line bottoms with wax paper; grease and flour paper.

2. Place contents of 1 package cake mix, 1¼ cups water, ⅓ cup vegetable oil and 2 eggs in large bowl; beat until blended. Place 1 cup batter in small bowl; stir in ¼ cup sugar and 2 tablespoons cocoa until blended. Divide vanilla batter evenly into prepared pans; spoon cocoa batter in dollops over top of batter in pans. With knife or spatula, marble chocolate through vanilla batter.

3. Bake 30 to 35 minutes or until wooden pick inserted in center comes out clean. Cool 15 minutes; remove cakes from pans. Remove wax paper; cool completely.

4. Repeat steps 1, 2 and 3.

5. Prepare Premier White Buttercream Frosting and Chocolate Buttercream Frosting. To assemble cake, cover 18×14-inch heavy cardboard with foil. Cut both round layers in half vertically. Arrange 1 square and 2 semi-circles into heart shape. Spread with small amount of frosting; place remaining square and 2 semi-circles on top. Frost top with white frosting; frost sides with chocolate frosting. Outline entire top and bottom edges of heart-shaped cake with Mini Kisses™ Chocolates. Garnish with Milk Chocolate Filigree Hearts, if desired.
Makes 24 servings

continued on page 270

Shower Them with Kisses Cake

Shower Them with Kisses Cake, continued

Premier White Buttercream Frosting

1⅔ cups (10-ounce package) HERSHEY'S Premier White Chips
 ⅓ cup milk
1½ cups (3 sticks) cold butter, cut into pieces
1¾ cups powdered sugar

1. Place white chips and milk in large microwave-safe bowl. Microwave at HIGH (100%) 1 minute; stir. If necessary, microwave an additional 30 seconds at a time, until mixture is melted and smooth when stirred; cool to lukewarm.

2. Beat butter and powdered sugar gradually into white chip mixture; beat until fluffy.

Makes about 4 cups frosting

Chocolate Buttercream Frosting: In bowl, place 2 cups of Premier White Buttercream Frosting; beat in 2 tablespoons HERSHEY'S Cocoa.

Milk Chocolate Filigree Hearts

1 cup HERSHEY'S MINI KISSES™ Milk Chocolates

1. Draw desired size heart shapes on paper; cover with wax paper. Place both sheets of paper on baking sheet or tray.

2. Place Mini Kisses™ Chocolates in microwave-safe bowl. Microwave at HIGH (100%) 30 seconds or just until chocolate is melted when stirred.

3. Pour melted chocolate in small, heavy seal-top plastic bag. With scissors, make small diagonal cut in bottom corner of bag. Pipe thick outlines of heart shapes following heart outlines; fill in center of hearts with a crisscross of chocolate to connect the sides. Refrigerate until firm.

4. Carefully peel wax paper away from chocolate hearts. Place on tray; cover and refrigerate until ready to use as garnishes for cake.

Leprechaun Cupcakes

**1 package (about 18 ounces) yellow or white cake mix plus
   ingredients to prepare mix
1 container (16 ounces) vanilla frosting
   Green, orange and red gumdrops, assorted candies and black
   decorator gel**

1. Preheat oven to 350°F. Place paper liners in 24 (2½-inch) muffin pan cups.
Prepare cake mix according to package directions. Spoon batter into prepared cups,
filling ⅔ full.

2. Bake 15 to 20 minutes or until toothpicks inserted into centers come out clean.
Cool in pans on wire racks 10 minutes. Remove from pans to racks; cool completely.

3. For leprechaun hats, sideburns, beards and mouths, roll out large green, orange or
red gumdrops on generously sugared surface. Trim pieces to look like hat, sideburns,
beards and mouths as shown in photo. Pipe decorator gel over seam for hat band.
Place candies on hat band as buckle and on face as eyes.   *Makes 24 cupcakes*

tip

Food colorings are edible dyes, usually red, green,
blue and yellow, used to tint frostings and candies.
The most popular type are liquid colors available
at supermarkets. Paste colors, which are sold at
specialty stores, come in a wider variety of colors
and are well suited to foods that do not mix well with
liquid. Both types impart intense color and should
initially be used sparingly, a drop or two at a time.

Leprechaun Cupcakes

Big Cheek Bunny Cake

**1 package (18¼ ounces) cake mix (any flavor), plus ingredients to
   prepare mix**
   Fluffy White Frosting (recipe follows)
2 cups shredded coconut, tinted pink
2 purchased coconut-covered cupcakes
   Red string licorice
   Assorted candies
1 (15×10-inch) cake board, covered, or large tray

1. Preheat oven to 350°F. Grease and flour two 8- or 9-inch round baking pans.

2. Prepare cake mix according to package directions. Pour batter evenly into
prepared pans.

3. Bake 30 to 35 minutes or until toothpicks inserted into centers come out clean. Let
cool in pans on wire racks 10 minutes. Remove from pans to racks; cool completely.

4. Prepare Fluffy White Frosting. Cut out cake pieces from 1 cake round as shown
in Diagram 1. Position cakes on prepared cake board as shown in Diagram 2,
connecting pieces with small amount of frosting. Frost cake with remaining frosting;
sprinkle with coconut. Decorate with cupcakes, licorice and candies as shown in
photo. *Makes 12 servings*

Fluffy White Frosting: Combine 1 (16-ounce) container vanilla frosting and
¾ cup marshmallow creme in medium bowl; mix well. Makes about 2 cups frosting.

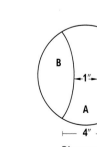

Diagram 1

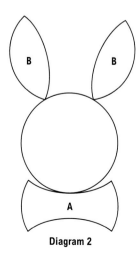

Diagram 2

Big Cheek Bunny Cake

Easter Egg Cake

2 packages (16 ounces each) pound cake mix
1 tablespoon finely grated lemon peel
1 bag (14 ounces) sweetened flaked coconut
¼ cup water
   Green food coloring
1 container (16 ounces) white frosting
   Pastel gumdrops

1. Preheat oven to 350°F. Spray 3-D egg cake pans* with cooking spray and dust with flour. Place baking rings on baking sheet and top with pans.

2. Prepare both cake mixes according to package directions; stir in lemon peel. Pour batter equally into cake pans; level batter. Bake on middle rack of oven 40 to 45 minutes or until cakes test for doneness. Cool in pans on wire racks 15 minutes. Remove cakes from pans; cool completely on wire racks.

3. Place coconut in large resealable plastic food storage bag. Combine water and food coloring in small bowl until of desired shade; sprinkle over coconut. Seal bag; shake until coconut is evenly tinted. Set aside.

4. Trim flat sides of cakes using long, serrated knife. Place baking ring in center of serving platter. Position bottom half of cake on ring, flat side up. Spread frosting over flat surface. Top with remaining cake half, aligning edges and ends to form egg shape. Frost cake.

5. Decorate cake with gumdrops as desired. Sprinkle tinted coconut around base of cake. *Makes 8 to 12 servings*

Available at specialty shops, in baker's catalogs, and online.

Banana Pudding Cake

Cake
> **1 package (about 18 ounces) spice cake mix**
> **1⅓ cups water**
> **⅓ cup vegetable oil**
> **3 eggs**
> **1 teaspoon vanilla, butter & nut flavoring or vanilla extract**
> **1 ripe banana, peeled and mashed (½ cup)**

Topping
> **1 cup cold whipping cream**
> **⅓ cup powdered sugar**
> **1 teaspoon vanilla**
> **4 ounces cream cheese, softened**
> **1 package (3.4 ounces) instant vanilla pudding and pie filling mix**
> **1¼ cups milk, divided**
> **½ teaspoon ground nutmeg**
> **1 ripe banana**
> **8 to 10 fresh flowers, stems removed (optional)**

1. Preheat oven to 350°F. Lightly grease 2 (8-inch) square cake pans; line bottoms of pans with waxed paper.

2. For cake, combine cake mix, water, oil, eggs and flavoring in medium bowl; beat until well blended. Add mashed banana; mix well. Pour into prepared cake pans. Bake 30 minutes or until toothpicks inserted into centers come out clean. Cool in pans on wire racks 15 minutes. Remove cakes from pans; cool completely.

3. For topping, place whipping cream in medium bowl; beat 1½ to 2 minutes or until soft peaks form. Add powdered sugar and vanilla; beat until stiff peaks form. Combine cream cheese, pudding mix and ¼ cup milk in large bowl; beat until well blended. Add remaining 1 cup milk and nutmeg; beat until smooth. Fold in whipped cream. Cover with plastic wrap; refrigerate until needed.

4. Place 1 cake layer on serving plate; spoon ¾ cup pudding mixture evenly over top. Slice banana; arrange evenly over cake. Top with remaining cake layer; top with remaining pudding mixture. For garnish, if desired, cut 7-inch circle from waxed paper. Lightly spray both sides of circle with nonstick cooking spray; place circle on top of cake. Arrange flowers on waxed paper as desired. Remove flowers and waxed paper before serving.
Makes 12 servings

Dad's Necktie Cake

**1 package (18¼ ounces) cake mix (any flavor), plus ingredients to
    prepare mix**
1 container (16 ounces) cream cheese or vanilla frosting
Blue and green food colorings
Assorted candies (optional)
Yellow decorating icing
1 large tray or (15×13-inch) cake board, covered
Pastry bags, medium star tip and small writing tip

1. Preheat oven to 350°F. Grease and flour 13×9-inch baking pan.

2. Prepare cake mix according to package directions. Pour batter into prepared pan.

3. Bake 30 to 35 minutes or until toothpick inserted into center comes out clean.
Cool in pan on wire rack 10 minutes. Remove from pan to rack; cool completely.

4. Cut out cake pieces as shown in Diagram 1. Position pieces on tray or prepared
cake board as shown in Diagram 2, connecting pieces with small amount of frosting.

5. Remove ¾ of the frosting from container; place in small bowl. Tint with blue food
coloring. Tint remaining frosting in container with green food coloring.

6. Frost cake with blue frosting. Spoon green frosting into pastry bag fitted with
star tip; pipe decorations on tie as desired. Decorate with candies, if desired. Spoon
yellow icing into second pastry bag fitted with writing tip; pipe desired message onto
cake. *Makes 12 servings*

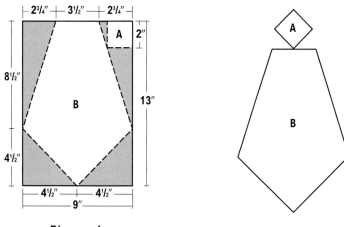

Diagram 1   **Diagram 2**

Dad's Necktie Cake

Firecrackers for the Fourth

3 packages (18¼ ounces each) pudding-in-the-mix cake mix (any flavor), plus ingredients to prepare mixes
3 empty 6-ounce aluminum cans, washed, dried and both ends removed
2 cups strawberry spreadable fruit
3 containers (16 ounces each) vanilla frosting
  Red and blue paste food coloring
  Black string licorice
1 tube (4¼ ounces) white decorator icing with tips

1. Prepare cake mix according to package directions. Reserve 1 cup batter. Divide remaining batter among 2 (9-inch) square baking pans and 4 (7½-inch) square disposable baking pans. Generously grease and flour cans. Cover one end of each can tightly with aluminum foil. Pour about ⅓ cup reserved cake batter into each can. Place filled cans on baking sheet.

2. Bake according to package directions. Cool in pans and cans 10 minutes. Remove from pans and cans to wire racks; cool completely. Wrap tightly in plastic wrap; freeze overnight.

3. Trim 2 (7½-inch) cakes to 5-inch squares. Spread one 5-inch cake, one 7½-inch cake and one 9-inch cake with ⅓ cup spreadable fruit each; top each with remaining same-sized cake.

4. Place 1½ containers frosting in medium bowl; tint with red food coloring. Place ½ container frosting in small bowl; tint with blue food coloring. Frost sides of 9-inch cake with red frosting; frost top with white frosting. Frost 1 side of 7½-inch cake with blue frosting; frost remaining sides with white frosting. DO NOT FROST TOP. Frost 1 side of 5-inch cake with blue frosting; frost remaining sides with red frosting and frost top with white frosting. Frost can cakes one each with red, white and blue frosting.

5. Place 9-inch cake on serving platter. Top with 7½-inch cake, turning at angle to the right. Frost top right corner of 7½-inch cake with blue frosting as shown in photo. Frost remaining top of middle layer with white frosting. Place 5-inch cake on top, twisting to the right at same angle.

6. Add firecrackers to cake top, cutting ends at angles as necessary. Place remaining frosting in small resealable plastic food storage bags. Cut off tiny corner of each bag; pipe onto firecrackers as desired. Place small piece of licorice in each firecracker for fuse. Pipe border around base and top of cake, and up sides with white decorator icing.
Makes 30 servings

Firecrackers for the Fourth

Batty Pumpkin Cake

1 package (18¼ ounces) spice cake mix
1 cup water
½ cup solid-pack pumpkin
⅓ cup vegetable oil
3 eggs
2 teaspoons pumpkin pie spice*
1 container (16 ounces) dark chocolate frosting
   Halloween cake decorations and colored icings

Substitute 1 teaspoon ground cinnamon, ½ teaspoon ground ginger and ¼ teaspoon each ground allspice and ground nutmeg for 2 teaspoons pumpkin pie spice.

1. Preheat oven to 350°F. Grease and flour 13×9-inch baking pan.

2. Combine cake mix, water, pumpkin, oil, eggs and pumpkin pie spice in large bowl. Beat at low speed of electric mixer 1 minute; scrape side of bowl. Beat at medium speed 2 minutes. Spoon batter into prepared pan; smooth top.

3. Bake 32 to 35 minutes or until toothpick inserted into center comes out clean. Cool 10 minutes on wire rack. Remove cake from pan; cool completely on wire rack.

4. Trim top and sides of cake. Cut cake as shown in Diagram 1. Place piece A on large serving platter. Attach piece B with some frosting as shown in Diagram 2. Trim wing edges to be rounded, if desired. Frost entire cake with remaining frosting. Decorate with cake decorations and icings as desired.   *Makes 12 to 16 servings*

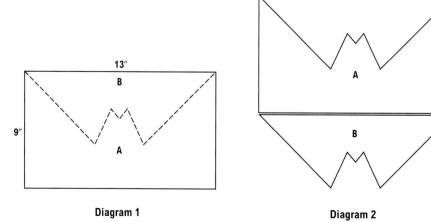

Diagram 1

Diagram 2

Batty Pumpkin Cake

Magical Wizard Hats

1 package (18¼ ounces) cake mix (any flavor), plus ingredients to prepare mix
2 containers (16 ounces each) white frosting
Yellow and purple or black food colorings
2 packages (4 ounces each) sugar cones
Orange sugar, decors and black decorating gel

1. Line 24 standard (2½-inch) muffin pan cups with paper baking liners. Prepare cake mix and bake in muffin cups according to package directions. Cool in pans on wire racks 15 minutes. Remove cupcakes from pan; cool completely on wire racks.

2. Frost cupcakes. Place ½ cup remaining frosting in small bowl; tint with yellow food coloring. Tint remaining frosting with purple or black food coloring.

3. Spread sugar cones with dark frosting, covering completely. Place 1 cone upside down on each frosted cupcake. Spoon yellow frosting into small resealable plastic food storage bag. Cut off small corner of bag. Pipe yellow frosting around base of each frosted cone. Decorate as desired. *Makes 24 cupcakes*

Wolfman Cake

1 package (18¼ ounces) cake mix (any flavor), plus ingredients to prepare mix
1 container (16 ounces) chocolate frosting
1 container (16 ounces) caramel frosting
Assorted candies such as candy corn, gummy worms and jelly beans
Black and red decorating gels

1. Prepare cake mix and bake according to package directions in 13×9-inch baking pan. Cool in pan on wire rack 15 minutes. Remove cake from pan; cool completely.

2. Cut cake in half crosswise to make two 6½×4½-inch layers. Place 1 layer on serving platter. Spread ½ of chocolate frosting over bottom layer. Top with second layer. Spread remaining chocolate frosting over top and sides of cake.

3. Spoon caramel frosting over top of cake. Use back of spoon to pull frosting out in fluffy "furry" tips. Decorate face with assorted candies and decorating gels as desired.
Makes 12 servings

Magical Wizard Hats

Witchy Spice Cake with Cherries & Pecans

Cake
- ½ **cup dried cherries**
- ½ **cup apple juice**
- 1 **package (18¼ ounces) spice cake mix, plus ingredients to prepare mix**
- ½ **cup coarsely chopped pecans, toasted**

Frosting
- 1 **package (8 ounces) cream cheese, cut into chunks**
- ¼ **cup butter, cut into chunks and softened**
- 2 to 2½ **cups powdered sugar**
- 1 **teaspoon vanilla**
- **Witch stencil**
- **Colored sugar**

Cake

1. Preheat oven to 350°F. Grease two 9-inch round cake pans.

2. Combine cherries and apple juice in small microwavable bowl. Microwave at HIGH about 1 minute or until apple juice bubbles. Set aside.

3. Prepare cake mix according to package directions. Drain cherries. Stir cherries and pecans into cake batter. Spread batter evenly in prepared pans. Bake about 35 minutes or until toothpicks inserted into centers come out clean. Cool in pans on wire rack 15 minutes. Remove cakes from pans; cool completely on wire racks.

Frosting

4. Place cream cheese and butter in bowl of food processor fitted with steel blade. Add 2 cups powdered sugar and vanilla. Pulse just until well blended. If frosting is too stiff, process additional 10 seconds. If frosting is too soft, add additional powdered sugar. Frost top of one cake; place second layer on top. Frost both layers. Place stencil on top of cake; sprinkle colored sugar over stencil. Lift stencil to reveal design. *Makes 16 servings*

Witchy Spice Cake with Cherries & Pecans

Ooze Cupcakes

1 package (8 ounces) cream cheese, softened
½ cup powdered sugar
⅓ cup thawed frozen limeade concentrate
1 teaspoon vanilla
   Yellow and blue food coloring
1 package (18¼ ounces) chocolate cake mix
1 egg
   Water and vegetable oil
1 container (16 ounces) vanilla frosting
   Orange sugar

1. Preheat oven to 350°F. Line 24 standard (2½-inch) muffin pan cups with paper baking liners, or spray with nonstick cooking spray.

2. Combine cream cheese, powdered sugar, limeade concentrate and vanilla in large bowl; beat until well blended. Tint with yellow food coloring; beat until well blended. Set aside.

3. Prepare cake mix according to package directions using 1 egg, water and oil. Spoon batter into prepared muffin cups, filling half full. Spoon 1 rounded teaspoon cream cheese mixture in center of each cup.

4. Bake about 20 minutes or until toothpicks inserted into centers come out clean. Cool completely on wire racks.

5. Add 4 drops yellow food coloring and 2 drops blue food coloring to frosting. Stir until well blended; adjust color as needed by adding additional food coloring 1 drop at a time, blending well after each addition. Spread frosting on cooled cupcakes. Sprinkle with sugar. *Makes 24 cupcakes*

Ooze Cupcakes

Scaredy Cat Cake

1 package (18¼ ounces) devil's food cake mix, plus ingredients to prepare mix
1 container (16 ounces) dark chocolate fudge frosting
4 individual square chocolate snack cakes
1 large orange gumdrop
   Granulated sugar
   Black decorating gel
   Black string licorice, cut into 3½- to 4-inch lengths
2 large yellow gumdrops

1. Prepare and bake cake mix according to package directions in two 8-inch round baking pans. Cool in pans on wire rack 15 minutes. Remove cakes from pans; cool completely on wire rack.

2. Place one layer upside down on serving platter; frost top with chocolate frosting; add second layer right side up. Frost entire cake with chocolate frosting.

3. Cut snack cakes in half diagonally. Frost tops of all snack cake triangles. Make 2 stacks of 4 triangles each. Place at top of round cake for ears; frost to blend in with round cake. Use back of spoon to pull frosting on sides of cake out in "furry" tips.

4. Roll out orange gumdrop on generously sugared surface. Cut out large triangle; place in center of cake for nose. Use black gel to draw mouth. Place licorice on face for whiskers.

5. Roll out yellow gumdrops on generously sugared surface. Cut out pointed ovals; place on cake for eyes. Pipe gel onto eyes for pupils.   *Makes 12 servings*

Scaredy Cat Cake

Spider Cupcakes

1 package (18¼ ounces) yellow or white cake mix
1 cup solid-pack pumpkin
¾ cup water
3 eggs
2 tablespoons vegetable oil
1 teaspoon ground cinnamon
1 teaspoon pumpkin pie spice*
   Orange food coloring
1 container (16 ounces) vanilla, cream cheese or caramel frosting
4 ounces semisweet chocolate
4 dozen black gumdrops

Substitute ½ teaspoon ground cinnamon, ¼ teaspoon ground ginger and ⅛ teaspoon each ground allspice and ground nutmeg for 1 teaspoon pumpkin pie spice.

1. Preheat oven to 350°F. Line 24 standard (2½-inch) muffin pan cups with paper baking liners, or spray with nonstick cooking spray.

2. Combine cake mix, pumpkin, water, eggs, oil, cinnamon and pumpkin pie spice in large bowl. Beat at medium speed of electric mixer 3 minutes or until well blended.

3. Spoon ¼ cup batter into each muffin cup. Bake about 20 minutes or until toothpicks inserted into centers come out clean. Cool 10 minutes on wire rack. Remove cupcakes from pan; cool completely.

4. Add orange food coloring to frosting. Stir until well blended; adjust color as needed by adding additional food coloring 1 drop at a time, blending well after each addition. Frost cupcakes.

5. Place chocolate in small resealable plastic food storage bag. Microwave at MEDIUM (50% power) 40 seconds. Knead bag; microwave 30 seconds to 1 minute or until chocolate is melted. Knead bag until chocolate is smooth. Cut off tiny corner of bag. Drizzle chocolate in four or five concentric circles over top of one cupcake. Immediately draw 6 to 8 lines at regular intervals from center to edges of cupcake with toothpick or knife to make web. Repeat with remaining cupcakes and chocolate.

6. For spider, place one gumdrop in center of web design on top of cupcake. Roll out another gumdrop with rolling pin. Slice thinly and roll into "legs." Place legs onto cupcake to complete spider. Repeat with remaining gumdrops and cupcakes.

Makes 24 cupcakes

Spider Cupcakes

Turkey Cupcakes

1 package (18¼ ounces) cake mix (any flavor), plus ingredients to prepare mix
1 container (16 ounces) chocolate frosting
¾ cup marshmallow creme
24 shortbread ring cookies
2 sticks white spearmint gum
48 small red candies
Candy corn and assorted candies for decoration

1. Preheat oven to 350°F. Line 24 standard (2½-inch) muffin pan cups with paper baking cups.

2. Prepare cake mix according to package directions. Spoon batter into prepared muffin cups.

3. Bake 15 to 20 minutes or until toothpicks inserted into centers come out clean. Cool in pans on wire racks 10 minutes. Remove from pan to wire racks; cool completely.

4. Combine frosting and marshmallow creme in medium bowl; mix well. Frost cupcakes lightly with frosting mixture; reserve remaining frosting mixture.

5. Cut cookies in half. Cut 24 halves in half again to form quarters.

6. For each cupcake, stand 1 cookie half upright on back edge of cupcake for tail. Place 1 cookie quarter on opposite side of cupcake for head; reserve remaining cookie quarters for another use. Frost cookies with remaining frosting mixture to blend in with cupcake.

7. Cut gum into ¼-inch pieces; trim both ends of gum into points. Fold gum in half to form beaks; place on bottom edges of heads. Position candies on heads for eyes. Decorate tops of tails with candies as desired.   *Makes 2 dozen cupcakes*

Hanukkah Cookies

Cookies
    ¾ cup butter or margarine, softened
    2 egg yolks
    2 tablespoons grated orange peel
    1 package DUNCAN HINES® Moist Deluxe® White Cake Mix

Frosting
    1 container (16 ounces) DUNCAN HINES® Vanilla Frosting
    3 to 4 drops blue food coloring
    3 to 4 drops yellow food coloring

1. For cookies, combine butter, egg yolks and orange peel in large bowl. Beat at low speed with electric mixer until blended. Add cake mix gradually, beating until thoroughly blended. Form dough into ball. Cover with plastic wrap and refrigerate for 1 to 2 hours or until chilled but not firm.

2. Preheat oven to 375°F.

3. Roll dough to ⅛-inch thickness on lightly floured surface. Cut with Hanukkah cookie cutters. Place 2 inches apart on ungreased cookie sheets. Bake at 375°F for 6 to 7 minutes or until edges are light golden brown. Cool 1 minute on cookie sheets. Remove to cooling racks. Cool completely.

4. For frosting, tint ½ cup Vanilla frosting with blue food coloring. Microwave at HIGH (100% power) for 5 to 10 seconds, if desired. Place writing tip in pastry bag. Fill with tinted frosting. Pipe outline pattern on cookies. Tint ½ cup frosting with yellow food coloring and leave ½ cup frosting untinted; decorate as desired. Allow frosting to set before storing between layers of waxed paper in airtight container.

Makes 3½ to 4 dozen cookies

Dreidel Cake

1 package (18¼ ounces) cake mix (any flavor)
1¼ cups water
3 eggs
¾ cup sliced or slivered almonds, toasted and finely ground
¼ cup vegetable oil
½ teaspoon almond extract
1½ containers (16 ounces each) cream cheese frosting
   Yellow and blue food colorings
   Pastry bag and medium star tip

1. Preheat oven to 350°F. Grease and flour 13×9-inch baking pan.

2. Mix cake mix, water, eggs, almonds, oil and extract in bowl. Beat at low speed of electric mixer until blended. Beat at medium speed 2 minutes. Pour into prepared pan.

3. Bake 35 to 40 minutes or until toothpick inserted into center comes out clean. Cool in pan on wire rack 10 minutes. Remove from pan; cool completely on rack.

4. Trim rounded cake top, if necessary. Cut cake as shown in Diagram 1. Position cake pieces on large tray or covered cake board as shown in Diagram 2, connecting pieces with small amount of frosting. Frost center of cake with about ½ cup white frosting.

5. Tint about ¾ cup frosting desired shade of yellow with food coloring. Spread onto top and sides of cake as shown in photo.

6. Using Diagram 3 as guide, cut out pattern from waxed paper; position on cake. Trace around pattern with toothpick; remove pattern. Tint remaining frosting blue. Spoon frosting into pastry bag fitted with star tip. Pipe stars to fill in symbol and pipe border around top edge of cake as shown in photo.   *Makes 12 servings*

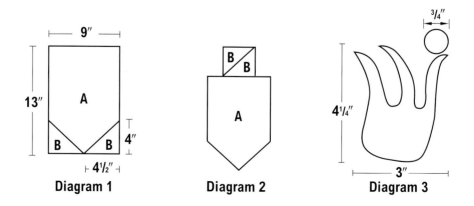

Diagram 1   Diagram 2   Diagram 3

Dreidel Cake

Ribbon Cake

Cake
- **1 package DUNCAN HINES® Moist Deluxe® Classic White Cake Mix**
- **¼ cup flaked coconut, chopped**
- **¼ cup natural pistachio nuts, finely chopped**
  Green food coloring
- **¼ cup maraschino cherries, drained, finely chopped**
  Red food coloring

Filling and Frosting
- **3¼ cups confectioners' sugar**
- **½ cup shortening**
- **⅓ cup water**
- **¼ cup powdered non-dairy creamer**
- **1½ teaspoons vanilla extract**
- **¼ teaspoon salt**
  Green food coloring
- **½ cup natural pistachio nuts, finely chopped**
- **¾ cup cherry jam**
  Whole maraschino cherries with stems and mint leaves for garnish

1. Preheat oven to 350°F. Grease and flour three 8-inch square cake pans.

2. For cake, prepare cake mix following package directions for basic recipe. Combine 1¾ cups batter and coconut in small bowl; set aside. Combine 1¾ cups batter, pistachio nuts and 5 drops green food coloring in small bowl; set aside. Combine remaining batter, ¼ cup chopped maraschino cherries and 2 drops red food coloring. Pour batters into separate pans. Bake at 350°F for 18 minutes or until toothpick inserted in center comes out clean. Cool following package directions. Trim edges of cakes.

3. For filling and frosting, combine confectioners' sugar, shortening, water, non-dairy creamer, vanilla extract, salt and 5 drops green food coloring in large bowl. Beat for 3 minutes at medium speed with electric mixer. Beat for 5 minutes at high speed. Add more confectioners' sugar to thicken or water to thin as needed. Add remaining ½ cup pistachio nuts. Stir until blended.

4. To assemble, spread green and white cake layers with cherry jam. Stack layers. Top with pink layer. Frost sides and top of cake. Garnish with whole maraschino cherries and mint leaves. *Makes 12 to 16 servings*

Hint: To save time, use Duncan Hines® Creamy Homestyle Vanilla Frosting. Tint with several drops green food coloring.

Ribbon Cake

Snowman Cupcakes

1 package (about 18 ounces) yellow or white cake mix, plus ingredients to prepare mix
2 containers (16 ounces each) vanilla frosting
4 cups flaked coconut
15 large marshmallows
15 miniature chocolate covered peanut butter cups, unwrapped
Small red candies and pretzel sticks for decoration
Green and red decorating gels

Preheat oven to 350°F. Line 15 standard (2½-inch) muffin pan cups and 15 mini (¾-inch) muffin pan cups with paper baking cups. Prepare cake mix according to package directions. Spoon batter into prepared muffin cups.

Bake 10 to 15 minutes for mini cupcakes and 15 to 20 minutes for large cupcakes or until cupcakes are golden and toothpicks inserted into centers come out clean. Cool in pans on wire racks 10 minutes. Remove from pans to racks; cool completely. Remove paper baking cups.

To assemble, frost bottoms and sides of large cupcakes; coat with coconut. Repeat with mini cupcakes. Attach mini cupcakes to large cupcakes with frosting for snowman bodies. Attach marshmallows to mini cupcakes with frosting for snowman heads. Attach inverted peanut butter cups to marshmallows with frosting for snowman hats. Use pretzels for arms and small red candies for buttons as shown in photo. Pipe faces with decorating gels as shown. *Makes 15 snowmen*

Snowman Cupcakes

Festive Fudge Blossoms

¼ cup butter, softened
1 package (18¼ ounces) chocolate fudge cake mix
1 egg, lightly beaten
2 tablespoons water
¾ to 1 cup finely chopped walnuts
48 chocolate star candies

1. Preheat oven to 350°F. Cut butter into cake mix in large bowl until mixture resembles coarse crumbs. Stir in egg and water until well blended.

2. Shape dough into ½-inch balls; roll in walnuts, pressing nuts gently into dough. Place about 2 inches apart on ungreased baking sheets.

3. Bake cookies 12 minutes or until puffed and nearly set. Place chocolate star in center of each cookie; bake 1 minute. Cool 2 minutes on baking sheets. Remove cookies from baking sheets to wire racks to cool completely.

Makes 4 dozen cookies

Prep and Bake Time: 30 minutes

tip

Warm nuts are easier to chop than cold or room temperature nuts. To warm them, place 1 cup of shelled nuts in a microwavable dish and microwave at HIGH about 30 seconds or just until warm; chop the nuts as desired.

Festive Fudge Blossoms

Reindeer Cupcakes

1 package (18¼ ounces) chocolate cake mix, plus ingredients to
   prepare mix
¼ cup (½ stick) butter, softened
4 cups powdered sugar
5 to 6 tablespoons brewed espresso
½ cup (3 ounces) semisweet chocolate chips, melted
1 teaspoon vanilla
   Dash salt
24 pretzel twists, broken in half
   Assorted candies for decoration

1. Preheat oven to 350°F. Line 24 standard (2½-inch) muffin pan cups with paper baking cups.

2. Prepare cake mix according to package directions. Spoon batter into prepared muffin cups. Bake 15 to 20 minutes or until toothpicks inserted into centers come out clean. Cool in pans on wire racks 10 minutes. Remove from pans to wire racks; cool completely.

3. Beat butter in large bowl with electric mixer at medium speed until creamy. Gradually add powdered sugar and 4 tablespoons espresso; beat until smooth. Add melted chocolate, vanilla and salt; beat until well blended. Add remaining espresso, 1 tablespoon at a time, until frosting is of desired spreading consistency.

4. Frost cooled cupcakes with frosting. Decorate with broken pretzel pieces for antlers and assorted candies for reindeer faces. *Makes 24 cupcakes*

Reindeer Cupcakes

Star Christmas Tree Cookies

Cookies
    ½ cup vegetable shortening
    ⅓ cup butter or margarine, softened
    2 egg yolks
    1 teaspoon vanilla extract
    1 package DUNCAN HINES® Moist Deluxe® Classic Yellow or Devil's
        Food Cake Mix
    1 tablespoon water

Frosting
    1 container (16 ounces) DUNCAN HINES® Creamy Home-Style Classic
        Vanilla Frosting
    Green food coloring
    Red and green sugar crystals for garnish
    Assorted colored candies and decors for garnish

1. Preheat oven to 375°F. For cookies, combine shortening, butter, egg yolks and vanilla extract. Blend in cake mix gradually. Add 1 teaspoonful water at a time until dough is rolling consistency. Divide dough into 4 balls. Flatten one ball with hand; roll to ⅛-inch thickness on lightly floured surface. Cut with graduated star cookie cutters. Repeat using remaining dough. Bake large cookies together on *ungreased* baking sheet. Bake 6 to 8 minutes or until edges are light golden brown. Cool cookies 1 minute. Remove from baking sheet. Repeat with smaller cookies, testing for doneness at minimum baking time.

2. For frosting, tint Vanilla frosting with green food coloring. Frost cookies and stack, beginning with largest cookies on bottom and ending with smallest cookies on top. Rotate cookies when stacking to alternate corners. Decorate as desired with colored sugar crystals and assorted colored candies and decors.

Makes 2 to 3 dozen cookies

Star Christmas Tree Cookies

Easy Egg Nog Pound Cake

1 (18.25-ounce) package yellow cake mix
1 (4-serving size) package instant vanilla pudding and pie filling mix
¾ cup BORDEN® Egg Nog
¾ cup vegetable oil
4 eggs
½ teaspoon ground nutmeg
   Powdered sugar, if desired

1. Preheat oven to 350°F. In large mixing bowl, combine cake mix, pudding mix, Borden Egg Nog and oil; beat at low speed of electric mixer until moistened. Add eggs and nutmeg; beat at medium-high speed 4 minutes.

2. Pour into greased and floured 10-inch fluted or tube pan.

3. Bake 40 to 45 minutes or until wooden pick inserted near center comes out clean.

4. Cool 10 minutes; remove from pan. Cool completely. Sprinkle with powdered sugar, if desired.   *Makes 1 (10-inch) cake*

Prep Time: 10 minutes
Bake Time: 40 to 45 minutes

Easy Egg Nog Pound Cake

acknowledgments

The publisher would like to thank the companies and organizations listed below for the use of their recipes and photographs in this publication.

Cherry Marketing Institute

Dole Food Company, Inc.

Duncan Hines® and Moist Deluxe® are registered trademarks of Aurora Foods Inc.

Eagle Brand® Sweetened Condensed Milk

Filippo Berio® Olive Oil

Hershey Foods Corporation

Kahlúa® Liqueur

© Mars, Incorporated 2005

McIlhenny Company (TABASCO® brand Pepper Sauce)

Mott's® is a registered trademark of Mott's, LLP

Nestlé USA

Northwest Cherry Growers

The Quaker® Oatmeal Kitchens

The J.M. Smucker Company

index

metric conversion chart

VOLUME MEASUREMENTS (dry)

$\frac{1}{8}$ teaspoon = 0.5 mL
$\frac{1}{4}$ teaspoon = 1 mL
$\frac{1}{2}$ teaspoon = 2 mL
$\frac{3}{4}$ teaspoon = 4 mL
1 teaspoon = 5 mL
1 tablespoon = 15 mL
2 tablespoons = 30 mL
$\frac{1}{4}$ cup = 60 mL
$\frac{1}{3}$ cup = 75 mL
$\frac{1}{2}$ cup = 125 mL
$\frac{2}{3}$ cup = 150 mL
$\frac{3}{4}$ cup = 175 mL
1 cup = 250 mL
2 cups = 1 pint = 500 mL
3 cups = 750 mL
4 cups = 1 quart = 1 L

VOLUME MEASUREMENTS (fluid)

1 fluid ounce (2 tablespoons) = 30 mL
4 fluid ounces ($\frac{1}{2}$ cup) = 125 mL
8 fluid ounces (1 cup) = 250 mL
12 fluid ounces (1$\frac{1}{2}$ cups) = 375 mL
16 fluid ounces (2 cups) = 500 mL

WEIGHTS (mass)

$\frac{1}{2}$ ounce = 15 g
1 ounce = 30 g
3 ounces = 90 g
4 ounces = 120 g
8 ounces = 225 g
10 ounces = 285 g
12 ounces = 360 g
16 ounces = 1 pound = 450 g

DIMENSIONS

$\frac{1}{16}$ inch = 2 mm
$\frac{1}{8}$ inch = 3 mm
$\frac{1}{4}$ inch = 6 mm
$\frac{1}{2}$ inch = 1.5 cm
$\frac{3}{4}$ inch = 2 cm
1 inch = 2.5 cm

OVEN TEMPERATURES

250°F = 120°C
275°F = 140°C
300°F = 150°C
325°F = 160°C
350°F = 180°C
375°F = 190°C
400°F = 200°C
425°F = 220°C
450°F = 230°C

BAKING PAN SIZES

Utensil	Size in Inches/Quarts	Metric Volume	Size in Centimeters
Baking or Cake Pan (square or rectangular)	8×8×2	2 L	20×20×5
	9×9×2	2.5 L	23×23×5
	12×8×2	3 L	30×20×5
	13×9×2	3.5 L	33×23×5
Loaf Pan	8×4×3	1.5 L	20×10×7
	9×5×3	2 L	23×13×7
Round Layer Cake Pan	8×1½	1.2 L	20×4
	9×1½	1.5 L	23×4
Pie Plate	8×1¼	750 mL	20×3
	9×1¼	1 L	23×3
Baking Dish or Casserole	1 quart	1 L	—
	1½ quart	1.5 L	—
	2 quart	2 L	—